Issues in the Social Sciences Series: 6

Series Editors: Anne Boran and David Charles Ford

Poverty: Malaise of Development

In the Same Series

1. *Crime: Fear or Fascination?* edited by Anne Boran

2. *Gender in Flux;* edited by Anne Boran and Bernadette Murphy

3. *Decoding Discrimination;* edited by Mark Bendall and Brian Howman

4. *Implications of Globalisation;* edited by Anne Boran and Peter Cox

5. *Fragmenting Family?;* edited by David Charles Ford

6. *Poverty: Malaise of Development;* edited by Anne Boran

7. *Cont_texts? Media, Representation and Society;* edited by Meriel D'Artrey

Poverty: Malaise of Development

*Papers from a conference held at the
University of Chester
November 2005*

Edited by Anne Boran

Chester Academic Press

First Published 2010
by Chester Academic Press
University of Chester
Parkgate Road
Chester CH1 4BJ

Printed and bound in the UK by the
LIS Print Unit
University of Chester
Cover designed by the
LIS Graphics Team
University of Chester

The introduction and editorial material
© University of Chester, 2010
The individual chapters
© the respective authors, 2010

All Rights Reserved
No part of this publication may be reproduced, stored in a retrieval system or transmitted in any form or by any means without the prior permission of the copyright owner, other than as permitted by UK copyright legislation or under the terms and conditions of a recognised copyright licensing scheme

A catalogue record of this book is available
from the British Library

ISBN 978-1-905929-79-5

CONTENTS

Contributors   vii

Foreword   xi

Acknowledgements   xiii

Introduction   1
Anne Boran

1. "Poverty" as a Malaise of Development: A Discourse Analysis in its Global Context   33
Wendy Olsen

2. Critical Perspectives on Issues of Global Poverty   66
Robert Biel

3. Child Poverty in a Developing World   93
Shailen Nandy

4. Unaffordable Risks and Unaffordable Protection: How Poverty Reduction Programmes and Food Security Strategies Can Undermine Each Other   127
David Hall-Matthews

5. Ethnicity, Poverty and Trade Liberalisation: The Khmer People in Southern Vietnam   161
Kirsten Besemer

6   Faith Matters: Development and the   198
    Complex World of Faith-Based
    Organisations
    Gerard Clarke

CONTRIBUTORS

Dr Wendy Olsen works as Senior Lecturer in Social Science Research Methods in the Institute for Development Policy and Management at the University of Manchester. She is the author of *Rural Indian Social Relations* (Oxford, 1996) and co-author of *The Politics of Money* (Pluto, 2002, with Hutchinson and Mellor). She has published papers on critical realism in the *Journal of Development Studies*, 2006, *Journal for the Theory of Social Behaviour*, 2005, and *Journal of Critical Realism* 2007 and 2008. She wrote an entry on *Poverty* for the *Dictionary of Critical Realism* (Routledge; Ed. M. Hartwig, 2007). In Salford, Wendy is on the management committee of a local centre for unemployed people. She visits India for her fieldwork, where she speaks Telugu. She is particularly interested in normative themes in social research (*Journal of Economic Methodology*, 2006). Her recent research project 2002-2007 within the Global Poverty Research Group (www.gprg.org/pubs/workingpapers) offered a Bourdieuvian re-interpretation of Indian rural peoples' labouring strategies.

Robert Biel is Senior Lecturer at the Development Planning Unit, University College London. He directs the M.Phil./Ph.D. programme there, having previously served as course director of the Master's course in Development Administration and Planning. Before joining UCL, he lectured at Birkbeck College and the School of Oriental and African Studies, both in the University of London. He has researched and taught about International Relations theory, the foreign relations of China, and various aspects of development theory, notably international political economy. Robert Biel is author of *The new imperialism* –

Poverty: Malaise of Development
Crisis and contradictions in North-South relations (Zed Books, 2000), a new revised edition of which appears in Spanish and Arabic in 2006, and of several more recent papers which coalesce around a common theme of the approaching crisis phase of a global capitalist system characterised by increasing environmental decay and militarism.

Shailen Nandy is currently doing a Ph.D. at the School for Policy Studies at the University of Bristol. He is examining trends in child poverty in developing countries between 1995 and 2005. Between 1999 and 2004 he worked as a researcher in the School on projects for UNICEF, the World Health Organisation and UK Department for International Development (DFID). He is currently involved in a DFID-funded study of adult, youth and child poverty in developing countries and lectures on poverty and development to students taking Master's degrees in Policy Research and Public Policy. His main interests are in poverty measurement and analysis, malnutrition and international development.

Dr David Hall-Matthews is a Senior Lecturer in International Development at the University of Leeds. His contemporary research has developed in two directions: the politics of food security and obstacles to effective states in southern Africa (particularly Malawi) and the political economy of development in India and South Asia. His research interests include the changing nature of Indian hegemony, corruption, democracy and the role of donors and the impact of globalisation on governments. Publications include: *Peasants, famine and the state in Colonial Western India.* (Palgrave Macmillan, 2005) and contributions to edited volumes 'Tickling Donors and Tackling Opponents: The Anti-Corruption Campaign in

Contributors

Malawi.' In S. Bracking (Ed.) *Corruption and Development: The Anti-Corruption Campaigns*, (Palgrave Macmillan, pp. 77-102, 2007), and Globalisation and the Role of the British State. In D. Brack, R. Grayson and D. Howarth (eds.) *Reinventing the State: Social liberalism for the 21st century*, (Politico's, pp. 175-194. 2007).

Kirsten Besemer is a Ph.D. student at the University of Chester, and she also works as a visiting lecturer in Development Studies. Originally from the Netherlands, she has lived and worked in various countries in Asia, including China, Japan and Vietnam. Her Ph.D. research explores the social effects of trade liberalisation in the Mekong River Delta of Vietnam, and is based on mixed-method fieldwork research.

Dr Gerard Clarke is Senior Lecturer in Development Studies in the Centre for Development Studies, School of the Environment and Society, Swansea University. His main research interests cluster around NGOs, civil society and development, especially in South-East Asia. He is the author of *The politics of NGOs in South-East Asia: Participation and protest in the Philippines* (Routledge, 1998) and co-editor, with Michael Jennings, of *Development, civil society and faith-based organisations*, Palgrave Macmillan, forthcoming. He has also worked as a consultant on international development issues to a range of organisations including the Department for International Development, the National Audit Office and the World Bank.

Anne Boran (editor) is a Senior Lecturer and Head of Department of Social and Communication Studies at the University of Chester. Her particular lecturing and research interests are in the areas of international political

Poverty: Malaise of Development

economy, globalisation and social movements. She worked in Sao Paulo, Brazil over a period of 10 years where she helped to set up the Movement for the Defence of Favelados (shanty town dwellers) in the east of Sao Paulo concerned with land rights, basic facilities and so forth. She became series editor of the *'Issues in the social sciences series,'* published by Chester Academic Press and her publications include *Crime: Fear or Fascination?*, *Gender in Flux*, Co-ed. Bernadette Murphy (Chester Academic Press, 2002) and *Implications of Globalisation*, Co-ed. Peter Cox (Chester Academic Press, 2007).

FOREWORD

The Millennium Development Goals (MDGs) and campaigns such as 'Make Poverty History' have placed poverty reduction at the centre of global development efforts at the start of the 21st century. This focus has moral dimensions in that there is widespread agreement that everyone has the right to a basic standard of living and quality of life. However, there is also the underlying belief that poverty acts as a brake on 'development' in all its forms. Thus, as the title of this book states, poverty can be seen as a malaise of development.

Paying attention to poverty is all well and good, but, as the contributors to this book highlight, doing something about poverty is a different matter. They bring out issues of definition and measurement, debates around causes of poverty and the complexities of poverty-alleviation policies.

Poverty can be defined in absolute terms, leading to efforts to identify a poverty line below which individuals are viewed as 'living in poverty', or alternatively engagement with ideas of social exclusion or inequality are associated with definitions of relative poverty. The book's contributors stress the multi-dimensional nature of poverty, reflected in the diversity of indicators and measures used. In particular, many contributors clearly demonstrate that poverty is not confined to certain parts of the world; while measures used to assess poverty may differ, poverty is found in all regions of the global North, as well as the countries of the global South. Finally, it is important to acknowledge the growing attempts to understand how poverty is understood and experienced by those defined as 'poor' by externally-derived measures.

David Hall-Matthews, in his chapter on food security, turns the title of this book around asking whether

Poverty: Malaise of Development

'development is a malaise for those in poverty?' This highlights arguments made in many chapters of the book regarding the causes of poverty. While poverty is viewed by some theorists and policy-makers, not least those associated with modernisation or neoliberal theories, as a result of limited or absent development, structural interpretations take the view that poverty is inherently linked to forms of capitalist economic growth. According to these approaches, poverty alleviation policies as currently conceived, can be viewed as very small-scale efforts which do nothing to challenge wider processes of exclusion.

Regardless of the definitions of poverty or understandings of its causes, attempts to alleviate poverty at a range of scales are found throughout the world and involve a diversity of actors. However, explicit poverty-reduction policies often fail to achieve their goals. In many cases this is because policy-makers fail to recognise how policies such as income diversification or improved education levels, may be interpreted by the supposed 'beneficiaries' of the policy. The role of factors such as gender, ethnicity, religion and age must also be considered to ensure that policies are appropriate to the context, but also that they do not exacerbate existing forms of social inequality.

This engaging and wide-ranging book will help readers comprehend both the fluidity of poverty as a concept, but also the challenges facing individuals, households, communities and policy-makers seeking to reduce poverty levels. Such understandings are vital if socially-just and environmentally-sustainable forms of development are to be achieved in the future.

Katie Willis, Department of Geography, Royal Holloway, University of London, October 2009.

ACKNOWLEDGEMENTS

My thanks go to all who work hard to organise excellent conferences each year and to colleagues in the department for their dedication and academic rigour. Thanks to my supportive family, John and David.

Sincere appreciation to the authors included in this volume for their stimulating contributions to academic debate and to Katie Willis for her insightful foreword.

Sincere thanks to Peter Williams and Sarah Griffiths, Editorial Advisors of Chester Academic Press, for their invaluable help and support in preparing this volume for publication.

To those who continue the battle against poverty, whether as victims or crusaders, keep up the good fight!

Anne Boran

INTRODUCTION

Anne Boran

The notion that poverty is a malaise or sickness at the heart of development, eroding and weakening it, is one that is not normally engaged with in the development literature. On the contrary, poverty tends to be seen as a state of un-development, assuming macro proportions in some poorer developing countries and micro proportions in more developed ones. In the first case, it is supposed that it will be ameliorated with the great coming of "development" - to a greater or lesser extent depending on the model of development promoted. In the latter case, it is sometimes regarded as "natural" (the poor are always with us) owing to unequal ability, personal failure or cultural conditioning, all of which policy initiatives can potentially target.

This volume engages with three broad thematic areas, *theoretical discourses and policy implications, vulnerability and poverty* and *solutions to poverty*. This introduction will attempt to contextualise poverty discourses and situate the contributions of the authors within them. It grapples with the ways in which poverty depreciates and undermines development efforts, setting a challenge to thinkers and policy-makers to find ways of engaging with forms of development that could effectively eliminate poverty in the world.

1. Theoretical discourses and policy implications

Theoretical perspectives attempt to analyse reasons for the existence and persistence of poverty and to provide solutions through the models proposed. In the post-World

Poverty: Malaise of Development

War 2 period, the favourite with development thinkers was modernisation theory. It presented Western development as an ideal to be aspired to and attempted to provide steps to attaining this, based primarily, but not exclusively, on capitalist economic strategies fuelled by industrialisation and technological diffusion. Western-style political and cultural patterns were believed to mark a progression from traditional "poor" to modern "developed" societies. Poverty might temporarily increase while investment accelerated, it was argued, but inevitably benefits would trickle down to the masses. The malaise, from this perspective, was the backwardness associated with traditional societies and the structures that constrained them. In the post-war period, economic development, inspired by such thinking, did indeed take off in many developing countries, but this was not accompanied by greater equality or a reduction in poverty for the masses.

The West, led by Britain, produced a middle way in the post-war era which was to become a model of interventionism, based on capitalism rather than socialism. Influenced by the ideas of the economist John Maynard Keynes, it provided a response to the failures of the classical *laissez faire* economics that dominated 18th and early 19th century life. In this period wealth creation and the problem of poverty were believed to be resolved by the market and individualism. The global shocks of two world wars and a major depression sharpened the appetite for change, not least because of the growing appeal of communist ideology to the working-class poor. Keynesian social interventionist strategies combined commitment to both capitalist economic growth and to state-funded welfare. Capitalism could be made servant to a higher purpose, it was argued; that of distribution. The state played a central role in economic life by bringing key industries and services, such as transport and the utilities,

Introduction

under public ownership. Others remained in the private sector. Social objectives, such as full employment and welfare goals, were set. Keynesianism was optimistic about the ability of the state to manipulate spending and taxation in a way that would balance economic wealth creation and the welfare of its citizens. Poverty under such systems was seen as a constraint, but one that could be managed through the Welfare State and access to education, health care and benefits. This model produced economic growth, better welfare and living conditions, for the population until the latter half of the 1970s and inspired interventionist policies elsewhere.

In the 1970s, dependency theorists reacted with a stinging critique of the failures of modernisation strategies to deliver development to poor countries. Although economic growth increased in countries such as Brazil (at a rate of 10% per annum in the 1960s), this was accompanied by a greater polarisation of wealth rather than by decreasing poverty. In many Latin American countries, modernisation was also accompanied by dictatorships rather than by democratic political systems. Western models, therefore (according to dependency theorists such as Gunder Frank in Latin America, and Walter Rodney in Africa), instead of being emulated, should be rejected. They were responsible, they argued, for intensifying poverty, exploitation and underdevelopment through the mechanisms of colonialism, imperialism and multinational company activities (used to extract wealth and resources for use in the West). This same process of wealth extraction and impoverishment, it was argued, continues to be facilitated through the policies and power of global financial institutions such as the World Bank and the International Monetary Fund [IMF]. Consequently, socialist, state-centred approaches that would de-link developing countries from the West would serve

Poverty: Malaise of Development

underdeveloped countries better. This, it was argued, would produce a more even development, where poverty might be eliminated.

The developmental state, whether inspired by socialist, military or capitalist ideals is, however, expensive. In developing countries economic development tended to be debt-led and in the developed world, in times of economic downturn, welfare was debt-supported. Loans were drawn from the private banking sector and from global financial institutions (the World Bank and the IMF) funded by national governments. The debt crisis reached global proportions by the late 70s and 80s, driven by the OPEC [Organisation of Petroleum Exporting Countries] instigated oil crises. State centred solutions to wealth creation and poverty alleviation were replaced by neoliberal market solutions that put the responsibility for success or failure firmly on the individual rather than on society or the state. Under what became known as the Washington Consensus, neoliberal thinking dominated economic and development policy from the 1980s onwards, facilitating globalisation and making a particular impact on both wealth creation and rising poverty levels during this time.

As contributors to this volume so ably highlight (see particularly Olsen and Biel in relation to this), and as this brief sketch of different approaches to understanding development and poverty asserts, outcomes for the poor are directly affected by strategies based on particular ideological understandings. From the 1980s, poverty shifted into sharp focus as an ongoing malaise, detracting from development successes such as the BRIC [Brazil, Russia, India and China] economies.

Introduction

What is poverty?

Poverty as a malaise presents not just a single face to the world but multiple and complex ones. It can be glimpsed in the records of non-achievers at school in the West or encountered fully in images of hunger and famine in the developing nations. A more obvious face may be the haphazard shelter offered by the massive shanty towns in many growing Third World cities and the struggle for basic health in the face of lack of sanitation, clean water and access to health services in many rural and urban areas. Much of the world has become accustomed to the shocking message that, in some parts of the world it is a privilege to survive beyond the age of five years. In Sierra Leone the under-five infant mortality rate was 26.8% in the poorest 20% of the population in 2005 (United Nations Development Programme [UNDP], 2007, p. 286). We have also grown used to the loss of whole generations of economically active men and women felled by AIDs (17.0% of the population aged between 15-40 years were HIV positive in Zambia in 2005 (UNDP, 2007, p. 280). Realities such as these shock and challenge us in a direct and uncompromising way.

Poverty, however, has a more subtle aspect. It can be glimpsed in the faces of the migrant, resented as a threat to the citizens of the host country. It can be recognised in the faces of those who have no say in the society in which they live, who lack basic freedoms or who fear for their lives - the faces of the socially excluded. There are different dimensions of poverty, some easy to identify, such as lack of income, food or shelter. Others are less immediately obvious but no less constraining, such as lack of education, poor job prospects, being of a particular gender, race or political/social group or even of a certain age - in other

Poverty: Malaise of Development

words the face does not quite "fit" within a given "orthodoxy".

According to the World Bank (2002), "poverty [is] defined as whether households or individuals have enough resources or abilities today to meet their needs". This approach to understanding and measuring poverty is based on consumption or income levels. The focus is on the material goods necessary to maintain life. A minimum level of income and consumption is set, below which an individual is held to be unable to satisfy basic needs. This minimum level is usually called the "poverty line". The idea that poverty was anything but the fault of the individual, pioneered by Booth and Rowntree at the turn of the 20th century in Britain, was strongly resisted by a society dominated by classical liberal economic thinking. Booth and Rowntree were able to demonstrate that income and consumption needs were not being met for a large part of the poor population, because of lack of jobs, inadequate wages, etc. This thinking helped to establish the concept of "absolute poverty" and set the scene for more liberal-minded governments to set targets to lift people out of poverty. Poverty lines were used to indicate acceptable and unacceptable levels of poverty.

The World Bank originally estimated the poverty line as $1 a day (for absolute poverty), and $2 a day (for slightly less acute poverty). In 1993, this corresponded more precisely to $1.08 and $2.25 respectively in Purchasing Power Parity [PPP] terms. PPP denoted equivalence in local currency purchasing terms. The poverty line is usually established by finding the total cost of what is regarded as the essential resources (including food needs and non-food needs) needed for a tolerable life for an average human adult in one year. The poverty line will be higher in developed countries, reflecting the higher costs of such provisions. Revisions to this poverty line were made

Introduction

by the World Bank in 2008, replacing the old line with a new one of $1.25, based on new baseline and new PPP figures for 2005 (Chen & Ravallion, 2008). Chen and Ravillion estimated that 1.4 billion people, or one quarter of the population of the developing world, lived below the new international line of $1.25 a day based on 2005 prices; 25 years earlier, in 1980, there were 1.9 billion poor, or one half of the population based on the earlier poverty line. This indicated an overall decrease in poverty across the world. The poverty rate in East Asia fell from almost 80% to under 20% over this period. By contrast, it stayed at about 50% in sub-Saharan Africa, though with signs of progress since the mid 1990s according to the authors.

Raising the poverty line causes much debate about earlier estimates of numbers in poverty. This is because this can appear to suggest either an increase or decrease, and hence positive or negative news about what is happening to poverty. For example, Chen & Ravallion (2008), using the new 2005 baseline, found that 204 million Chinese people were poor in 2005, about 130 million more than previously thought. However, further analysis by Ravallion, Chen & Sangraula (2008) estimated that, as China had based its figures on eleven cities, rural purchasing power was underestimated (rural prices tend to be lower). Their recalculations, to take account of this, suggest that poverty declined from 84% in 1981 to 22% in 2004, a decline of 62% (rather than the 53% of the former estimates) - a 9% difference in the numbers lifted out of poverty. This would support the view that, at least for the growth economies such as China and India (in relation to which similar issues were raised) real poverty levels have declined. However, as noted earlier, evidence is hotly debated and is dependent on the poverty line adopted and on how calculations are conducted across national economies (Bretton Woods Project, 2008). For a detailed

Poverty: Malaise of Development

critique of poverty lines and the calculations of Ravallion et al. see Subramanian (2009).

In order to establish a hierarchy of economic development, the World Bank ranks countries in the world by Gross National Product [GNP].[1] By averaging each country's GNP (i.e. dividing the total by the population), a notional figure of individual earnings is arrived at, called per capita GNP. This makes comparisons between countries straightforward and enables judgements to be made about levels of development across the world. Useful information about levels of economic development, and particularly about the gap between rich and poor countries in terms of the financial resources at their disposal, can be gleaned from this measure. Figures for 2005 demonstrate that the per capita GDP of Iceland was $53,290 per annum, whereas that of Lesotho was $808. It tells us little about how the fruits of development are actually spent by governments (for example, in 2005, Lesotho spent 13.4% of its GDP of $1.5 billion on education, while Iceland spent 8.1% of $15.8 billion (UNESCO, 2007/8), p. 266-267). Lesotho's level of commitment of resources to education is impressive, given the high numbers in poverty (36.4% live on less than $1 a day and 56.1% on less than $2 a day). As a consequence of resource commitment to education, the adult literacy in 2005 was 82.2%. This says much about Lesotho's commitment to improving the quality of life of its citizens, but also of the limitations poverty imposes on nations.

Per capita GNP also tells us little about how resources are divided among citizens of each country (which is worth

---

[1] GNP is the total of goods and services produced by a country, given a monetary value, added to earnings raised by exports, interest on loans made by that country and remittances from its citizens working abroad. Finally payment for imported goods and services and interest paid on debt owed externally are subtracted to calculate the GNP.

Introduction

noting when it comes to a discussion of relative poverty) or about the non-monetary quality of life of the people. There is some logic in thinking that economic development creates conditions for poverty alleviation and social inclusion, but that it will do so in practice is not a foregone conclusion. Further examination of countries with similar per capita GNP levels shows varying ranges of economic distribution and different levels of wealth control by sectors in society. Brazil and Republic of Korea have similar GDP levels, $796.1 and $787.6 billions respectively, yet distribution levels are quite different. The poorest 20% of the Brazilian population get just 2.8% of the national income as opposed to 7.9% in the Republic of Korea. The richest 20% of Brazilians share a substantial 61.1% of the national income, Republic of Koreans share only 37.5%. Therefore, distribution is far more even in the case of the Republic of Korea (UNESCO, 2007/8, p. 281).

Social dimensions /indicators of poverty

As can be observed from the above, some progress has been made in terms of analysing income poverty in a way that allows us to compare within and across countries. As suggested earlier, a limitation of these analyses is that they do not capture other important dimensions of poverty, such as health, education and access to services and infrastructure; nor do they measure them. A wide variety of approaches are suggested by theorists and policy-makers to attempt to capture those qualities of life that constrain people in ways that limit their freedom and to create indices that attempt to measure them. For example, the World Bank has tried to access these dimensions in their "Voices of the Poor" research, which recognises the risks, vulnerability, social exclusion and powerlessness to which the poor are exposed. Such approaches assume that

Poverty: Malaise of Development

poverty means that a person is not free to lead a long, healthy, and creative life when denied access to a decent standard of living, freedom, dignity and the respect of others. This approach focuses on the causes of poverty and leads directly to strategies of empowerment to enhance opportunities for everyone. It implies that poverty must be addressed in all of its dimensions, not income alone.

One such measure that links neatly with this approach is the United Nations Development Programme's *Human Poverty Index* [HPI]. This was introduced into the *Human Development Report* in 1997, in an attempt to bring together the different features of deprivation in a composite index related to the quality of life. It led to an aggregate judgment on the extent of poverty within a community. Rather than measure poverty by income, the HPI uses indicators of the most basic dimensions of deprivation: a short life, lack of basic education and lack of access to public and private resources. The HPI is derived separately for developing countries (HPI-1) and selected high income OECD countries (HPI-2), to better reflect socio-economic differences and also the widely different measures of deprivation in the two groups.

The first dimension relates to survival: the likeliness of death at a relatively early age. It is represented by the probability of not surviving to ages 40 and 60 respectively for the HPI-1 and HPI-2 groups. The second dimension relates to knowledge: being excluded from the world of reading and communication. This is measured by the percentage of adults who are illiterate. The third dimension relates to a decent standard of living; in particular, overall economic provisioning.

For the HPI-1 group, the third dimension is measured by the unweighted average of the percentage of the population without access to safe water and the percentage of children who are underweight for their age. For the HPI-

Introduction

2 group, the third dimension is measured by the percentage of the population below the income poverty line (set at 50% of median household disposable income). In addition to the three indicators mentioned above, HPI-2 also includes social exclusion as a fourth dimension. It is represented by the rate of long-term unemployment (United Nations Development Programme, 1997). Not surprisingly, the highest HPI scores are found in Africa, and the lowest in Japan. The fact that different indices are used for poorer and wealthier countries indicates recognition of the different relative poverty standards between them: i.e., that the poor are better off in richer countries and consequently, the malaise is not of standard proportions.

Because indices measuring the quality of life are in essence qualitative, they are notoriously difficult to measure. Comparisons are difficult between countries or regions that differ markedly in terms of culture, economy and way of life. Rural/urban differences may be masked by aggregated data. The data collected may suffer from inaccuracies, inconsistencies and gaps which might not be apparent in the reported statistics. As with all composite indicators in which several measures are combined, it is important to recognise that the final index may hide differences in the component variables. Thus areas or countries with markedly different profiles of poverty may end up with a similar index value. There is no universally accepted single measure of poverty. This is because identifying and defining the poor first of all involves ethical questions about how welfare is measured. Nations differ as to how statistics are collected and, even when some measurements allow for an individual's own judgment of well-being, this makes for difficulties in comparison or standardisation.

Poverty: Malaise of Development

Having examined theoretical approaches in a historical context, together with conceptual approaches to understanding, defining and measuring poverty, it is important to focus on how society engages with the poor and generates policies to address their plight. How are views of poverty shaped? According to Wendy Olsen in her chapter, ""Poverty" as a Malaise of Development: A Discourse Analysis in its Global Context", views of poverty, and responses to it, are shaped by various societal discourses. Olsen's paper examines three key poverty discourses, the charity discourse, the social-exclusion discourse, and the economic poverty discourse. Olsen takes issue with these discourses, finding them lacking in structuralist analysis, particularly in relation to class, gender and ethnic relations. She engages initially with the "shame" of poverty, something that is rarely touched on in poverty analysis. The label "poor", imposed by the "non-poor", tends to be constructed solely in economic terms, so that it becomes reductionist and profoundly disempowering. The reality and potentials of "poor" lives gets lost, she argues, in the construction of the "other" in the discourses of policy-makers and the public. A central problem is that the poverty discourse is generated by the "non-poor" and directed towards the problem "poor". They, though by definition part of the poverty discourse, are there as objects, rather than as designers of solutions to the problem. The discourses are used to incorporate the public and governments into giving, particularly to poor countries, through aid and "fair" trade.

Olsen explores attempts by NGOs and other agencies to refine discourses over time, through changing language and visual imagery, but finds that they still struggle not to objectify the poor. The social exclusion/inclusion debate centres on a notion of the poor as "not belonging" in a real sense, of not sharing equal citizenship with the non-poor.

Introduction

Poverty ensures that they do not fit in, that they have not got quite the same rights as others. Depending on the discourse adopted, this is because society is not democratic enough (the position in many EU countries), because the poor are not responsible enough (Conservative and New Labour discourse in the UK over the past 30 years) or because governments do not engage in "good governance" (seen to be an ongoing problem in the case of developing countries). In neoliberal discourse, the problem, and the solution, tend to become increasingly individualised. Inclusion could come through assuming responsibility: single parents could get a job; the sick could get back to work or retrain if necessary; developing countries could find market solutions and their citizens would then be less dependent on the state, etc. Underlying structural causes of poverty are ignored in these discourses.

Olsen identifies contradictions in these discourses and argues that a transformationalist discourse offers a more realistic way forward. This discourse involves both reflection and action directed at structural inequalities. This is more likely, she argues, to improve the chances of ridding society of poverty. For this reason, Olsen's paper raises a seminal question about the usefulness of structural frameworks in the analysis of poverty. She argues strongly for the necessity of engaging with structural analysis.

Robert Biel also approaches poverty from a structuralist position. According to Biel, in his chapter, "Critical Perspectives on Issues of Global Poverty", the notion of "Making Poverty History" has no place within the logic of capitalism, where poverty is seen as a means for gaining comparative advantage. Current preoccupations with its elimination, he argues, including the Millennium Development Goals [MDGs], because they focus on absolute poverty, sidestep the linkages between poverty, wealth creation and pauperisation. Taking a

Poverty: Malaise of Development

Marxist analytical perspective, Biel examines what he calls the entropy of capitalism, its inability to fuel itself sustainably and its tendency to deplete the source of its own order - labour/human capacity and ecological and environmental resources. This is why, in his view, the concept of relative poverty is so important, because it keeps a focus on class and on the relational nature of poverty to wealth and of the poor to the wealthy. Assumptions cannot be made, therefore, that by growing the economy, poverty can be eroded and both rich and poor can improve their positions. This is because of the finiteness of resources.

Biel argues that top-down strategies to eliminate poverty emanating from the ruling order will tend to pre-empt, rather than tackle, the most effective means of dealing with poverty. Negative externalities, generated by the individual pursuit of profit maximisation, were recognised and moderated through social policy of the Keynesian type in the past, when regulation attempted to make capitalism work for everyone. This was only possible, Biel argues, because of the exportation of pauperisation to the South. More recently neoliberalism has effectively questioned the need for such policy interventions at all (emphasising, on the contrary, that the "nanny state" should be rolled back). Biel argues that a deep form of regulation moves entropy from one sphere to another, across structural divides such as gender, race, geographic divisions, etc. Pauperisation under capitalist development is shifted around spheres, in dependency theory terms, from core to periphery, from formal to informal sectors and away from core wealthy countries. It works, facilitated by globalisation, while there is capacity to absorb and supply cheap commodities, but at huge environmental costs. Commoditisation is fed, through the elimination of traditional features of societies, including

Introduction

those that help to sustain the poor such as common land ownership, free water, seeds and medicines. International institutions, imbued with neoliberal fervour are complicit in these processes. In this scenario, in order to address poverty, incomes must raise the standard of living of the poor and also compensate for those goods formerly available free of charge.

Profit maximisation and regulation of externalities, such as pauperisation, are in direct conflict with each other. It risks, Biel argues, an increasing descent into disorder, the "war on terror" representing an example of this. This is why, according to Biel, it is so important to focus on relative poverty - which is not to say that absolute poverty does not also need to be eliminated. A means of addressing this is through social action by the oppressed; action in which the real voices of the poor (in class terms) can be heard, rather than those of the powerful in their reflections on poverty.

As Biel's analysis highlights, ideological positions, together with the frameworks for analysis emanating from them, shape the policies that impact on poverty. Structuralist analysis links the untrammelled pursuit of profit to impoverishment, a linkage that is pertinent to the post-2008 economic crisis generated by the banks, when even the most prudent of market players faced impoverishment and the whole global financial system risked paralysis. Market players depended on State intervention to bail them out and the dominant economic and development orthodoxies came under scrutiny and were found to be wanting.

2. *Vulnerability and poverty*

The share of resources of some relative to others makes a difference to the possibilities of life, as Biel's chapter points

Poverty: Malaise of Development

out. This is true, not only of the developing, but also of the developed, world in which the percentage of income spent on addressing vulnerabilities may be less (as in the case of Iceland's expenditure on education relative to that of Lesotho's), but the actual amount of wealth spent tends to be much greater. Likewise, the gap between the very high earners and poor earners in any society skews averages, and does not give a true picture of the sheer wealth commanded by some, and the poverty experienced by others. The concept of relative poverty[2] is an interesting one. It is a relational one, determined by societal structures.

In Brazil, Dona Lili, a resident of a favela on the outskirts of Sao Paulo, is one of the poorest 10% of the population that share just 0.9% of the GDP, whereas Dona Luisa, one of the richest 10%, lives in a posh jardim (garden) area of the city and commands a share of 51.3% of the country's wealth. Their lifestyles will reflect this disparity in the share of national income. Dona Lili lives in a makeshift shack with no running water or electricity, and works long hours as a maid in the house of Dona Luisa. Dona Luisa lives with her banker husband in a beautiful house with maids and a guard at the gate. The family also has a house in the country and one by the beach in Sao Sabastiao (typical of the wealthy in Brazil). Dona Lili's children will have to be self-sufficient. She rises at 5.30 a.m. to clean her home, prepare food for her husband and family, get the household up and ready for the day ahead and do the washing, before leaving to do more of the same for her rich employer. Her address is a barrier to access to good schools for her children, and to employment for her

---

[2] Relative poverty refers to the standard of living of the poor in a society relative to the overall standard of living of the particular society in which they are located. So the poor in a developed country may appear to be relatively well off in comparison to the poor in a developing country. It is closely associated with the concept of social exclusion.

Introduction

husband and herself. Poor wages prohibit the chances of living in an ordinary neighbourhood, in an ordinary house, with decent facilities. Life chances are severely constrained under these conditions, leading potentially to a cycle of deprivation (should sources of income suddenly dry up, owing to a family crisis, such as illness, for example). This can easily lead to structural poverty, out of which it is difficult, if not impossible, to climb. Families can be trapped within a "culture of poverty" which makes social mobility extremely difficult.

Dona Luisa experiences a different life. She has maids to do the housework and mind the children, so that she can work part-time as a psychologist. She helps to maintain her good looks and appearance by attending the health club several times a week for pampering and exercise. Her children go to private schools and will on go to university. They are cushioned by a life of privilege, and it is probable that they will at least maintain the lifestyle of their parents[3].

Comparisons of what is regarded as necessary for a reasonable life varies in time and place, and each country uses poverty lines which are appropriate to its level of development, societal norms and values. In the UK, Chester, a beautiful old walled city in the North West of England, cannot generally be regarded as poor or deprived. In comparison to other UK cities, it has relatively few districts that are in the high deprivation bracket. However, one area of one district, the Lache, is in the top 1% for income deprivation in the UK (Chester City Council, 2004, p. 7). Indices of Deprivation that are used to measure this go beyond the income poverty dimension "by focusing on unmet need, which is caused by a lack of resources of all kinds, not just financial" (*The English Indices*

---

[3] Material draws on author's experience in Brazil.

Poverty: Malaise of Development

of Deprivation; as cited by Chester City Council, p. 9).[4] Using as examples two categories, employment deprivation at 36% and income poverty at 55%, particularly as they impact on children (71% in poverty) and the old (44% in poverty), these statistics easily compare in absolute terms with high deprivation areas in the developing world (for example Namibia's unemployment rate for 2006 was 33.8%). In relative terms, they compare badly with other areas of Chester, with other cities in Britain and indeed with the unemployment rate of 5.3% in the UK as a whole (UNESCO, 2007/8).

Many quantitative measurements of poverty estimate relative poverty by setting a poverty line based on a percentage of average income within a particular society. In the UK, this is set at 60% of average incomes. Based on these measurements, it is calculated that, even in the UK, 13.2 million people, or 22% of the population, live in poverty (Oxfam, 2009).

There are three chapters in this volume that relate directly to vulnerability and poverty. Shailen Nandy's chapter considers childhood vulnerability to poverty, David Hall-Matthews focuses on rural smallholder poverty and food insecurity in Africa, and Kirsten Besemer on rural poverty, ethnicity, gender and religion in Vietnam.

Child poverty

A quotation attributed to Mahatma Gandhi states that "a nation's greatness is measured by how it treats its weakest members". Since none are more vulnerable in society than

---

[4] These include Income Deprivation, Employment Deprivation, Health Deprivation and Disability, Education, Skills and Training Deprivation, Barriers to Housing and Services, Crime, Living Environment Deprivation, and two other indices: Income Deprivation affecting children, and Income Deprivation affecting older people.

Introduction

children, progress in relation to child poverty does give us an indication of efforts being made to tackle poverty overall. Poverty in childhood matters especially, because this experience can deny children opportunities that will affect the rest of their lives. It matters because children are particularly vulnerable to exploitation and abuse and have special developmental needs and rights. Children within the family/household (e.g. adopted children, child domestic workers, girls in some cultures) may not have equal access to household resources or opportunities. Lastly, children in many societies are active contributors to household resources, so understanding the impact of poverty on them is important for helping them and their families and communities (Marshall, 2003).

Promises were made by the Labour Government to halve child poverty in Britain by 2010 and to eliminate it by 2020, but it is unlikely that either target will be met. It was one of the Millennium Development Goals [MDGs], a target for both developed and developing nations. Although some headway was made in the UK between 1997 and 2004 through the introduction of family credits and child-centred services, evidence suggests that this trend has been reversed in recent years (Hills, 2009). In an EU review of the 2006-08 national reports on strategies for social protection and social inclusion, Frazer (2008) identified large families and children with special needs as being, in almost all cases, at increased risk of poverty and in need of targeted action. Children in care and disabled children, Roma and unaccompanied immigrant children, were noted in several reports as being particularly vulnerable groups, in need of special attention. The report considered that measuring family household income as the sole indicator of child poverty is wholly inadequate but, nevertheless, is still a useful tool for monitoring, understanding and reducing poverty throughout the EU.

Poverty: Malaise of Development

Shailen Nandy, in his chapter, "Child Poverty in a Developing World", examines the issue of child poverty and its impact on the health and development of children. He argues for a more nuanced approach to measurement than that of household income. The chapter traces the evolution of those concerns about child poverty that have come to be enshrined in the UN Convention on the Rights of the Child. Although concerns about child welfare have assumed importance in the field of development policy, with goals and targets being set for its decrease, Nandy argues that the reduction in child poverty falls far short of any goals set internationally in both developing and developed countries. Accurate measurement is problematic, and Nandy discusses the nature of such measurements, and the solutions developed by researchers at the University of Bristol using data collected by major international research projects on poverty. Stringent operational thresholds of child deprivation were set in relation to seven areas, against which available data were evaluated.

Disturbingly, results suggest that over 1 billion children (or half the children in the developing world) suffered from one or more deprivation, and one in three suffered two or more deprivations and were classified as living in absolute poverty. In the developed world, the author drew on research using other criteria of deprivation and discovered a rise of child poverty in 16 developed nations. This suggests an urgent need for attention by policy-makers. Nandy suggests some ways forward to address the situation effectively. However, issues of causality are not looked at in this paper, and it is difficult to judge the efficacy of policies unless they are linked to a structural analysis.

Introduction

Rural poverty

The burden of poverty is spread unevenly throughout our world. It differs by region. Africa, Asia and South America have the greatest concentrations of poverty. Some countries suffer higher poverty levels than others and specific areas within countries may bear the brunt of poverty (Chirtereka, 2008). According to Chambers (1997), rural areas account for the majority of people living in absolute poverty and for half of the world's malnourished. It is anticipated that this is unlikely to change before 2040. Dependence on agriculture for a living, therefore, seems to be a key indicator of vulnerability to poverty. This is an issue of concern for development thinkers because agriculture has to meet a basic need that is crucial to our very survival – the need for food and nourishment. Part of the problem seems to lie in the way land ownership is structured, with too many people depending on too little land from which to make a viable living, while too few control too much land. Agriculture provides too little employment for those who do not own land, and it may be affected negatively by climatic factors, infrastructural problems, population intensity, size of landholding and government strategies. Agriculture must provide sufficient food to sustain the population and keep pace with population growth. How this is best done, however, is a subject of contention.

Poverty in Africa is predominantly rural, concentrated in the East, West and South, where the rate of decline into poverty is faster than that of population growth (Chirtereka, 2008). In Africa, a relational analysis might point to certain groups of rural inhabitants as predominantly suffering from poverty, with circumstances (or rather structures) preventing them from overcoming their vulnerability. These are small farmers, nomads,

Poverty: Malaise of Development

herders, the displaced, households headed by women and those dependent on wage labour. They are not only poor in terms of income, but in terms of literacy rates and life expectancy which consistently fall below national averages, while school drop-out rates and infant mortality are above the national average (Green, 2008). Similar groups, with local variations, can be found among the poorest in Asia and Latin America. Are there common factors that feed the malaise of rural poverty? One factor might be the legacy of colonialism, which structured ownership and production in ways that laid the foundations for post-colonial inequity and dependency. Post-independence factors may include rulers (military or otherwise) who have squandered resources on futile projects, ran up debt, enriched themselves, abused their people and mismanaged conflicts and disasters. Recent structural adjustment programmes imposed by the World Bank and the International Monetary Fund to manage debt crises in developing countries, have added to, rather than ameliorated, conditions of crisis. They have constrained and guided development agendas in ways that have proved contentious, particularly in Africa.

Market solutions have been central to structural adjustment policies and to those of donor agencies. David Hall-Matthews provides an analysis of the realities facing small farmers asked to engage in poverty reduction programmes in his chapter, "Unaffordable Risks and Unaffordable Protection: How Poverty Reduction Programmes and Food Security Strategies Can Undermine Each Other". It provides key insights into the kind of structural constraints that such strategies encounter in the context of rural Africa.

Taking as a starting point the limitations of top-down poverty-reduction strategies, in which donors talk down to the poor, Hall-Matthews examines an extreme

Introduction

consequence of poverty: starvation. He looks at the relationship between food security programmes and poverty reduction programmes in a small-scale African farmer context. Such programmes, he argues, can actually undermine each other when farmers are both poor and food insecure. Risk is at the heart of why this is so. When the poor are required to take a risk that can have a negative outcome - increased hunger in the case of the food insecure - they are risk averse. Government and development agencies may see this risk aversion (e.g. not opting to produce higher value cash crops) as backwardness, conservatism or inability to embrace entrepreneurial values. Food-insecure farmers, however, must take into account what they can afford to lose, particularly risks to essential assets that would threaten livelihoods. Such risks will be avoided at all costs, because they are the lifeline to future food security. Survival strategies, such as the diversification of income sources, storage of food, sale of non-productive assets, etc., will be pursued rationally, according to Hall-Matthews, in order to manage such risks and minimise their impact in times of famine. A strategy that transfers production from food to cash crops creates fewer opportunities to plan against crisis and may create shortages and higher food prices as a result. It is clear from Hall-Matthews's arguments that neither strategy is likely to succeed if poor farmers are not allowed a voice and the rationality of their reluctance to be involved in risk-based strategies is not recognised.

Hall-Matthews provides apt analyses of why markets, despite their potential for increased wealth, are made imperfect by a series of internal and external barriers. Several suggestions are made to provide more secure market opportunities, while at the same time being mindful of welfare. Malawi is presented as an initial example of how this might be done. Strategies employed to

Poverty: Malaise of Development

create food security in grains there also succeeded in creating market stability and indications of poverty reduction.

Ethnic minority status adds an additional layer of vulnerability to that of small farmer when exposed to market forces. Kirsten Besemer, in her chapter, "Ethnicity, Poverty and Trade Liberalisation: The Khmer People in Southern Vietnam", uses a livelihood-centred approach to uncover some of the mechanisms by which trade liberalisation has exacerbated existing ethnic inequality in the Mekong Delta, by increasing the importance of those assets which ethnic minorities lack. The paper argues that the marginalisation of the Khmer people is a consequence of a number of factors that place them at a disadvantage. They lack the factor endowments they need to cope with the changing economic climate, so trade liberalisation is likely to increase rather than decrease their marginalisation. The chapter examines the tangible and intangible assets of the Khmer ethnic minority and highlights some of the future implications of a widening, ethnic, poverty and landlessness, divide. Unless circumstances change, Besemer argues, increasing ethnic divisions are likely to lead to political instability, social unrest (of which there are already signs) and greater economic inequality.

Besemer concludes that, while the inequality of ethnic Khmer people is not caused by trade liberalisation, it intensifies existing inequalities based on ethnicity, gender and religion. Political institutions, she argues, need to look beyond cultural simplifications and address underlying inequalities, because vulnerability to marginalisation will be intensified during periods of economic reform. This chapter provides an example of how several "vulnerability" markers, such as small farmer, ethnic minority status, gender, religious and linguistic differences

Introduction

can interact to amplify the risk of poverty intensification and social exclusion.

3. *Solutions to poverty*

The reasons why malaise attaches to poverty are easy to understand, but difficult to address. While it is recognised that the chances of poverty alleviation are higher if economic growth takes place, there is no absolute link between the two. This depends on how the benefits are distributed and markets managed. The optimism that globalisation will automatically trickle wealth downwards is lessened when data relating to an emerging industrial nation such as India is considered. As Watkins, (2008) points out, the benefits of growth can be highly skewed with poverty levels falling more slowly than in other high growth economies such as Vietnam or Brazil. Child malnourishment in India is higher than in Ethiopia, and well above the African average of 28%. Watkins argues that Bangladesh is cutting child deaths at a faster rate (50% faster) than India; had the rates been the same, India would have had 200,000 more children alive in 2008. Some "trickle-down effect" has been noted in rural areas (in poor states in the north and in relation to rural labourers and low caste groups), but wealth has in the main been flooding into urban areas and middle-class suburbs. Improvements have not been made in immunisation rates (fewer than half of India's children are fully immunised) and gender inequalities are also still rife in India, with boys getting access to food and medicine before girls.

Millennium Development Goals

The current most favoured response by governments and development agencies to the malaise of poverty and

Poverty: Malaise of Development

continued uneven progress are the Millennium Development Goals [MDGs]. These goals try to judge progress by combining a more multi-dimensional qualitative approach to poverty with some quantifiable practical measurement. In September 2000, 189 countries signed the Millennium Declaration which led to the adoption of the MDGs. The MDGs are a set of eight goals, for which 18 numerical targets have been set and over 40 quantifiable indicators identified. The goals are to:

- Eradicate extreme poverty and hunger;
- Achieve universal primary education;
- Promote gender equality and empower women;
- Reduce child mortality;
- Improve maternal health;
- Combat HIV/AIDS, malaria, and other diseases;
- Ensure environmental sustainability;
- Develop a global partnership for development.

Each goal was seen to be important for development and together they would be mutually reinforcing. Achieving them would require the co-operation of developed and developing countries, citizens, NGOs, international financial institutions and states alike. Good, and accountable, governance would be promoted, alongside the protection of human rights and respect for the rule of law. With these commitments, poverty would, it was promised, be well on the way to becoming history. Some of the chapters have already commented on this approach and its limitations, but a comprehensive critique was formulated by Samir Amin (2006). He argued that the policies that generate poverty were not discussed, nor were alternatives formulated; and that the reduction in public expenditure and the privatisation of education were not

Introduction

examined in relation to achieving universal education - only access to education. Empowerment is measured solely by calculating the proportion of wage-earning women. Liberalisation, including extreme privatisation and respect for the "intellectual property rights" of transnational corporations, is assumed to complement poverty reduction. Liberalisation is seen to equate with entering into "partnership" with the developed world. Policy proposals for heavily indebted poor countries, he argues, impose a genuinely colonial tutelage. He accuses the West of being led by an imperialist triad (the USA, Europe and Japan) and of serving its own interests in the process of leading an attack on poverty.

NGOs and aid as part of the solution

Since the 1980s, in particular, much more emphasis has been placed on the role of Non-Governmental Organisations [NGOs] as mechanisms for delivering development and addressing poverty in place of the state. Neoliberalism inspired market-led approaches to development, and individual and agency approaches to poverty alleviation. NGOs were thought to be ideal for the role because they were close to grass roots analyses and commanded trust from a giving public. Thus, they were considered to be good at promoting "bottom-up" solutions to the problem of poverty alleviation and ideally such solutions could be funded through money channelled through NGOs by both governmental and public aid. The state could thus withdraw from welfare provision.

NGOs, because of grassroots connections, can "go native" and direct strong critiques at governments for their neglect of the poor. A report by Oxfam into poverty in the UK is an example of this (Oxfam, April 2009). As a result, Oxfam was accused of adopting a political role and of lobbying the government rather than developing projects to address poverty. Adequate analysis of aid and the activities of NGOs would require a separate book. The activities of "Live Aid", "Comic Relief" and similar events certainly inspire generosity from the public and a feeling that something can and is being done about poverty. The "real" faces of poor people move us and inspire us to part with our money but, as Olsen, Biel, Hall-Matthews and Besemer point out, the poverty discourses and solutions are generally not driven by the poor. The aid business is worth approximately $134,766 million (OECD figures for 2008) and it sustains thousands of workers and administrative systems throughout the world. In Africa alone, according to Holman (2005), it is used to buy the services of 100,000 expatriates, rather than indigenous African development workers, to the tune of $4 billion annually. These development workers, he suggests, must share the blame for development disasters in Africa.

Nevertheless, NGOs have a powerful influential voice that drives development policy. Gerard Clarke, in his chapter, "Faith Matters: Development and the Complex World of Faith-Based Organisations", argues that, when it comes to intervention by NGOs to reduce global poverty, faith matters more than would initially appear. In an analysis of the role of faith-based organisations [FBOs], Clarke demonstrates that they make a greater contribution to international development than non-faith-based NGOs. Using a five-fold typology, Clarke distinguishes between faith-based representative organisations or apex bodies, faith-based charitable or development organisations, faith-based socio-political organisations, missionary organisations and faith-based radical, illegal or terrorist organisations.

FBOs vary in the way they use faith to mobilise staff or supporters and in the degree to which expectations of a

Introduction

"faith dividend" underpins the work they do with beneficiaries and partners. Clarke argues that secular partners are unlikely to tolerate overt commitment by an FBO to a given faith group or to accept religious conversion as an organisational goal. The role of faith in the work undertaken by FBOs ranges from the mandatory to the non-relevant, depending on the organisation. Evidence from the USA suggests that, in the majority of cases, there is little difference in motivation between FBO activists and more secular ones, in the sense that broad humanitarian principles, rather than faith itself, underpin action. Evidence suggests, according to Clarke, that mainstream Christian and Islamic FBOs are concerned primarily with development needs, and that faith motivates them to be so, but that donors are sceptical of faith-based motivation and need convincing that there are no hidden agendas. Clark explores and contrasts the broad split between FBOs with no proselytising agenda and those that have overt ones, some of the development goals of which may be positive and some problematic for donors.

Official Western donors and secular NGOs may share misgivings about FBOs and the extent to which they represent agendas that are at odds with mainstream NGOs but, according to Clarke, they would do well to engage with them in building alliances and multi-stakeholder partnerships in the battle against global poverty. In this battle, faith matters a great deal, to very many of the world's citizens and donors.

There are no easy solutions to the malaise of poverty. What seems clear from this volume is that theoretical frameworks and the policy initiatives derived from them are underpinned by ideologies and values. They inform how the poor are treated and whether poverty will increase or decrease in society. The vulnerable in society, such as rural small farmers, ethnic minority groups and

Poverty: Malaise of Development

children will be in the forefront of those affected by economic strategies and policy initiatives. The impact of these need not necessarily be negative – outcomes depend on the particular discourses and policies that are employed. The fact that there are no easy solutions should not stop us seeking them and to that end this volume will, it is hoped, inspire continued dialogue and analysis.

References

Amin, S. (2006). The Millenium Development Goals: A critique from the South. *Monthly Review, 57 (*10), 1-15.

Bretton Woods Project. (2008, June 17). World Bank and poverty debates (II): Poverty reduction claims vindicated? *Critical Voices on the World Bank and the IMF, Update 61.* Retrieved August 11, 2009, from: http://www.brettonwoodsproject.org/art.561848

Chambers, R. (1997). *Whose reality counts?: Putting the first last.* London: ITDG.

Chen. S., & Ravallion, M. (2008). The developing world is poorer than we thought, but no less successful in the fight against poverty. *Policy Research Working Paper 4703*, Washington, DC: World Bank.

Chester City Council (2005). *Deprivation in Chester District; Key findings from the English indices of deprivation 2004.* Chester: Chester City Council.

Introduction

Chirtereka, C. (2008). The scourge of poverty in the 21st Century: The case of Africa. *Rajagiri Journal of Social Development. 4* (2), 108 -121.

Frazer, H. (January 2008). Ending child poverty within the EU: A review of the 2008-2010 National Strategy Reports on social protection and social inclusion. Brussels: Eurochild.

Green, D. (2008). *From poverty to power: how active citizens and effective states can change the world.* Oxford: Oxfam International.

Hills, J. D. C. (Writer) (2009). Today Programme, Poverty and inequality. UK.

Holman, M. (27-06-2005). Welcome to the aid business!, Retrieved February 3, 2009 from: http://www.opendemocracy.net/democracy-africa_democracy/NGO_2630.jsp

Marshall, J. (2003). CHIP Briefing 1: Children and poverty - some questions answered. Childhood Poverty Research Centre, UK.

Millennium Development Goals [MDGs] (2009), Retrieved February 3, 2009 from: http://www.millenniumgoals/pdf/MDG-Report-2009_Eng.pdf

Poverty: Malaise of Development

OECD (2008) *Development Aid at a Glance 2008 – Statistics by Region*, Retrieved February 3, 2010 from: www.oecd.org/de/dacstats

Oxfam. (April 2009). Close to Home: UK poverty and economic downturn. Oxford: Oxfam Publications, UK.

Ravallion, M., Chen, S., & Sangraula, P. (2008). Dollar a day revisited, *Policy Research Working Paper Series 4620*, Washington, DC: The World Bank, Development Research Group, Poverty Team.

Subramanian, S. (2009). "How many poor in the world?": A critique of Ravallion's reply. *Economic and Political Weekly, 44* (5), 67-71.

United Nations Development Programme (2007). Human development report. Retrieved February 3, 2010 from: http://hdr.undp.org/en/reports/global/hdr1997/

UNESCO. (2007/8). Human Development Index. Geneva: UNESCO.

Watkins, K. (2008, 29/7/2008 July, 2008,). India lags behind Ethiopia in child poverty. *Gulf-Times.com.*

World Bank, PovertyNet, Poverty measurement and analysis, Retrieved February 3, 2010 from: http://www.worldbank.org/poverty/

"POVERTY" AS A MALAISE OF DEVELOPMENT: A DISCOURSE ANALYSIS IN ITS GLOBAL CONTEXT

Wendy Olsen

In this chapter, a social constructivist approach to poverty discourses is combined with a realist approach to the causes of poverty. The constructivist element is seen in a practical analysis of texts using photos and quotations from development publications. A specific argument is set out: three main discourses in these texts, all relating to 'poverty', all tend to mask the real structural elements and relations that perpetuate poverty in capitalist society today. The three discourses I focus on are the charity discourse, the social exclusion discourse, and the economic poverty discourse. I criticise discourses that have contradictory notions embedded in them. Without meaning to disparage those discourses, I argue that they need to be augmented (and hence radically changed) by the addition of a structuralist element that recognises that some oppressive class, gender and ethnic relationships need urgently to be changed. I point out one specific performative contradiction to illustrate my critique. The chapter ends by offering a better moral reasoning strategy than the simplistic poverty discourses. Thus, I argue, a weak social constructivist approach to poverty discourses can be combined with a realist approach to the causes of poor/rich relations.

As a reader, you will have to decide how to deal with the three standard discourses yourself. As a realist, I tend to take a transformative approach: one that challenges existing discourses in ways that progressively help society

Poverty: Malaise of Development

to move forward. This can be called transformationalism (e.g. Langley and Mellor, 2002).

Introductory anecdote

I would like to introduce the chapter with an anecdote from my research in my own locality, Salford in Greater Manchester, where I have lived for 18 years. Salford has several electoral wards which are among the most deprived places in the whole of England and Wales, according to the Indicators of Multiple Deprivation [IMD], 2004. Salford, as a whole, is now an area selected for regeneration funds since it qualified as among the 88 most deprived and low-income areas in the country, according to the Labour Party, after it got into government in 1997. Detailed studies of local poverty were conducted, notably the IMD 2000 as well as its update in 2004. I was brought in during 2004 by members of the Salford Local Partnership. The Partnership is a mutual enterprise; it is sponsored by the regeneration funds of central government, and consists of voluntary participants and organisations from the charity, business, and local government sectors of the city. The Partnership paid for me to conduct a small local study, jointly with about a dozen local development workers. Much cooperation occurred and we shared our views about poverty as well as about research methods whilst this study got under way. In the end we studied property price movements, ward-level and small area IMD indicators, income levels by ward, documents about the management of the area, and detailed interview transcripts. These interviews, however, could not be mapped on to socio-demographic characteristics of respondents related to poverty. The local development workers insisted that any question on

"Poverty" as a Malaise of Development

occupation, income or expenditure levels be removed from the interview and that no face-sheet of socio-demographic details could be used if it contained these personal, private details. Income, they repeatedly told me, was a sensitive subject.

In other words, in a study of poverty they didn't want to make anybody reveal whether they were poor or not. It soon became evident who was, in fact, poor (in economic, social or political terms) but this initial restriction was very intriguing. It implied that the people I was working with had reservations about what they considered to be disparaging to any individual - i.e. even hinting that they were on a low income. Yet when I provided detailed ward-level income data, everyone was fascinated (one ward had an average household income of 600 pounds per week after housing costs, whilst several others were between 280 and 340 pounds per week *on average*). Inequality was evident between the wards. But no one wanted inequality to become explicit in a room full of physical people. Not only would it be embarrassing to oneself, I learned, but it was also considered embarrassing to embarrass anyone else in this way.

Looking back at older histories of the working class in the Northwest, I found that Robert Roberts had already described a similar approach to human dignity in his book *The Classic Slum* (1971). Roberts argued that a pretence of equal dignity for everyone was widespread. This discourse was only broken once someone was overtly a criminal or if one acted in a way that was regarded as disgusting in public. The pretence of equality, Roberts noted, was overlaid by delicate structurings of a hierarchy of social status. Status was achieved for instance by having a piano (noted also by Skeggs in her description of class/gender intersections (Skeggs, 1997). Other status markers in the 1910-1922 period included keeping the steps

Poverty: Malaise of Development

clean, having a polite mother at home, helping others out, being overtly religious, and so on (Roberts, 1971). Many of these forms of status were accessible even to those who are economically poor. In this way, some social status was achievable by all, and in spite of great inequality there were few rumblings of revolution in the district of Salford during the 1910-1922 period about which Roberts wrote.

From Roberts' and Skeggs' book, and the other northern England classics by Friedrich Engels (1892) and by George Orwell (2001), we learn that economic poverty does not necessarily imply social stigma or political exclusion. However, social stigma and political exclusion are likely to follow from the degradation that is often (but not always) associated with economic poverty. Ironic, isn't it then, that economic poverty continues to be very difficult to *ask about* in interviews in 2004?

Part of the explanation is that economically poor people are usually construed as the other. In English phrasings, statements about 'the poor' typically imply that the speaker is automatically designated as non-poor. It is rare indeed for 'poor' people to talk about other poor people as such. Indeed one could argue that many people do not want to have a debate about either the poor or poverty. For instance, the UK government under 'New Labour' did not want to have a discussion about poverty as such, but rather about wealth creation. Another buzz phrase in use is 'social protection'. 'Indices of multiple deprivation' were constructed. Deprivation would be construed as a failure to properly target and protect these areas. Social protection policies would include benefits and social support as well as pensions. In other words, by framing the scene a certain way, a positive light can be cast upon it, and especially upon the speaker or author. In this way, poverty disappears and something more pleasant –

"Poverty" as a Malaise of Development

such as meaningfully targeted action - miraculously appears. Iyengar (1990) explains that the framing of poverty affects the politics of poverty. Yapa (1996) presents issues of subjectivity and reality with regard to poverty, helping to clarify how poverty discourses work. The 'subjective' realm is the one mainly set up using mental and linguistic constructs.

The way poverty is construed is itself a process of social construction. Poor people are construed (often airbrushed) out of existence. Yet poor people do exist, and many of us have personally experienced poverty at given points in life and understand something of what such a life is like. Poverty is a reality for poor people. Many poor people live in Salford. But it's possible for them and others to collude in hiding the realities of their lives. Not only is the label hidden, but also the real day-to-day difficulties, the hard choices and suffering. In our study, we heard about the use of food stamps, of taking up free school meals, of ostracism and racism during our interviews. Yet always the stories were about 'other' people, 'those' people. Not us.

The social construction of poverty was described by Maia Green as having a long history (2006). Green traces the historical predominance and usage of 'poverty' through a variety of schools of thought. These include anthropology in its early decades, the big international institutions as they construe poverty, and more recent normative statements from 1990 onward by global actors. For example, in the context of a debate over supply-side economics and structural adjustment, the 'poor' are those whose talents are wasted through bad government. To better use these talents, market forces need to be liberalised, some say, and government corruption and waste would need to be reduced (e.g. Berg Report, 1981). This came to be known as the Washington Consensus on

Poverty: Malaise of Development

market-oriented development. This Consensus underpinned the Structural Adjustment programmes aimed at restructuring the economies of less-developed, poorer, countries and setting them on the path of market-led growth. Now we have the post-Washington Consensus; this new 'consensus' is a widely-held view that government itself is sometimes not the most efficient way to deliver services, but that the government can help where the services are in any case not delivered by markets. The post-Washington Consensus idea that you intervene "where there is market failure", also has radical critics (Fine, 2001). This new consensus again has its own particular way of slotting 'poverty' and the 'poor' into the discourse. Fine explains that to say that the poor lack social capital is to avoid discussing deeper structural class problems. Green argues that there is nothing essential to be seeking, in poverty, but only these twists and turns of social construction of poverty (Green, 2006). As an anthropologist, her view is that poverty is simply socially constructed; my view is that poverty is partly socially constructed but also partly real . Elsewhere, Green offers important advice to those who run governments, or international institutions (Green, 2002). Her advice is to focus on real social differentiation and to avoid glib overview statements when framing policy. This is good advice but does not do justice to the need for a radical overhaul of dominant conceptions of poverty. In fact it seems rather mildly reformist.

Discourse analysis

I will describe three discourses in some detail in this chapter. First it is important to set out what a discourse is. Discourses are combinations of communicative acts that fit

"Poverty" as a Malaise of Development

together. In society, generally, we have neoliberal discourse, Marxist discourse, radical feminist discourse and so on. Focusing concretely on poverty-talk, there are some images to take into account, apart from texts and documents (see Table 1). A detailed breakdown of the components of three discourses is hinted at in Table 2. I will define discourse and then explain (and critique) each of the three. This is great fun but it is best to conclude by constructing an alternative. I can only sketch out that alternative here – which I call a transformationalist analysis of development – but there are plenty of authors working in this area. These authors are generally known as the post-development school. The title refers mainly to being post-neoliberal, post-economism, and post-capitalist in what the authors seek. You can think these aspects over while I run through the existing, much more reformist, discourses.

Table 1: Typical images of poverty.

	Charity Discourse	Social Inclusion Discourse	Economics of Poverty Discourse
Typical Photo Images	Orphan, hungry child, wrinkled older person	Crowds, meetings, white and black people together	Summary bullet points of achievements
Typical Graphical Images	A form to fill in for donating money	Pie chart of voting percentages (voting being a liberal notion of inclusion)	Bar charts

A discourse is a context-specific local set of rules or norms that kick in when people are interacting or communicating (Fairclough, 2001). The local rules need not always be followed. But discourses do shape how we communicate about poverty. Thus we might label the poor; target the poor; help the poor; eradicate poverty (or try to); or complain about the creation of poverty. According to the discourse being used, you might be able to combine two to three of these activities. But you can't both 'target' the poor and 'be' poor at the same time! The targeter is implicitly separate from an isolable group called the poor. It is, at this deeper level of semantics, language in use, or ontology, that we say that the discourse is a set of rules. Poor people don't talk about poverty, as they are (by definition, within poverty discourse) too busy scratching out a living somewhere. The speaker about poverty is constructed as a heroic, non-poor, figure, who is doing something about a problem.

In discourse analysis, there is an awareness that text, talk and images all combine to give impressions which are recognised, by their usual audiences, as giving or affirming typical messages. In this chapter I will illustrate this using images of anti-poverty charity groups, for example. Some images are visual or graphic images, while others are words that act as metaphors. Fairclough wrote a useful review of how to conduct discourse analysis (Fairclough, 1992, 1995). Another volume by Chouliaraki and Fairclough puts this into the context of theories of late modernity (1999), a useful addition. But in poverty studies we don't want to just look at late modern Europe – we want a global analysis of discourse. Therefore we may need to revise our conception of discourse analysis.

Whatever the place of language, pictures are always an important part of discourses. Fairclough includes many pictures from advertising and newspapers, as well as brochures and other genres, in his books. Table 1

"Poverty" as a Malaise of Development summarises the types of photo images we expect to find in each of the three main poverty discourses.

Table 2: Discourse components for three typical poverty discourses.

	Charity Discourse	Social Inclusion Discourse	Economics of Poverty Discourse
Agents of Technologisation	Non-governmental organisations	State and civil society	Economists, entrepreneurs
Agents -types –labels	Givers, needy people, donors, orphans, refugees (the more oppressed the better)	Voters, citizens	Firms, Workers, Entrepreneurs
Assumptions about structure	Poor/rich relationship is one which creates a demand that rich donate to poor	Strong class awareness; strong awareness of ethnic, gender and other divisions	Nil, because atomistic. Each class role is one into which people can choose to join if they wish (e.g. via Dragon's Den)
Assumptions about human actualisation	Restricted for poor; enhanced by kind and altruistic giving of money, for non-poor	Stunting and deprivation are measurable effects of social exclusion	Money is a means to human happiness. Important to measure money earnings
Role of states	State is not sufficient	State is an important actor	State role varies

Poverty: Malaise of Development

Role of the UN	Assumes that UN fails	UN and EU may be important in setting up agreed frameworks of individual rights	UN role varies
Myths	"Giving Helps"	"Human Development" matters	"The Invisible Hand" of the market
Tropes	Every little bit helps	Low level of development; 'backward'	Invest in human capital
Symbols	Café Direct logo	Country flags	Money logos on bills
Typical Verbs	Contribute	Participate, voice	Earn, create wealth

The Charity Discourse of Poverty

In looking at Table 1, we notice that images in the charity discourse are especially photographical, and in Figure 1 I provide samples of these types of images. They are easily recognisable – in association with their text – as charity donation request images. Of course the discourse of charity is very complex and has sub-divisions. My first picture illustrates a common strand from earlier decades, in which a picture of a struggling or hungry child easily attracts our attention. In the 1990s there was concern that these images caused emotional burnout and a gradual desensitisation of western readers to the suffering of hungry people (Kinnick, Krugman, and Cameron, 1996). Today readers also find the images somewhat degrading for the poor person who is objectified in the picture (Wright, 2004) so in order to avoid this insult, we get something more like the second (middle) picture. Wark

"Poverty" as a Malaise of Development

says 'the most innocent-looking media images are sometimes the most sinister' (Wark, 1995). Here, the orphans look normal but are possibly African and not exactly cheerful. The associated text explains their problem – they are evidently children of people who have died of AIDS virus related diseases. This photo is less denigrating for the subject. Still it is noticeable that they don't get a caption, nor do the subjects in the photo get names attributed to them. The person is objectified. Some people say that the charity discourse tends to commodify the people on whose behalf the organisations work (Wright, 2004). Wright's closely argued paper on Café Direct advertisements, for example, reminds us that the people in advertisement cannot speak to/about us, nor can they see us; whereas we can see and talk about them. They remain anonymous. This is known as objectifying the person. Wright argues that it actually fetishises them, following up on Marx's critique of capitalism. Marx's notion of commodity fetishism refers to the perception of goods in terms of our relation with the goods or their prices, rather than our relation with the producers of the goods. Human relations (which are class relations), he says, are reduced to the relations between the consumer and the thing [the product]. When Marx wrote, in the period 1860 to 1880, this was a vastly innovative thing to say. Even today, it appears in sociology texts but is not widely recognised in popular society. The 'glamour' and fashion industries rest firmly upon a denial of the fetishisation of the person. Perhaps you can see how, in charity discourse, even if the images show a happy healthy child, the poor person is still objectified and depersonalised. They are also not the agent of action! In charity discourse, the important agents are the donors and the intermediaries. A third agent is the media person or advertising expert. But all the agency aspects are subdued, and the moral aspect is primary. One is supposed to feel obligated to donate to mitigate the harm seen in the photos.

Figure 1: Typical images from contemporary donor appeals in charity discourse.

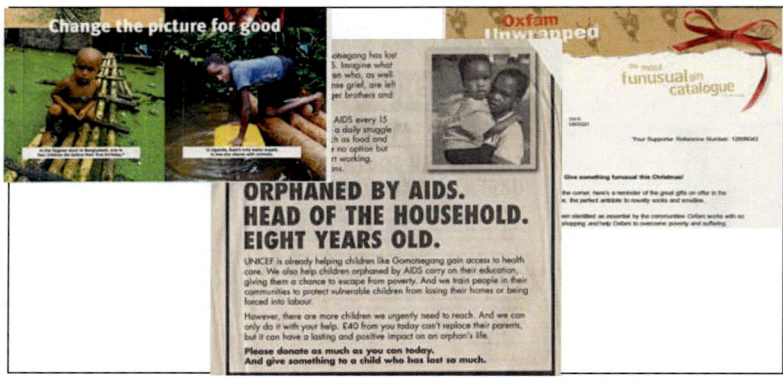

The third image in Figure 1 illustrates how Oxfam sometimes avoids having person-pictures. Instead we see a gift-wrap image. This is a massively consumerist image. Gift-wrapping is wasteful and luxurious. It involves producing a gift, which has symbolic meaning, by clothing it in layers of mystery and secrecy. The giving of the gift has further layers of symbolic meaning. Now we are seeing that a donation to charity can be perceived as a gift, to be given to a third party. The third party is going to get the message that waste is not approved of, but that spending has been done on their behalf. The third party is not going to receive a consumer good, but they will receive a message that the money has been spent on useful goods. The specific sentence used here to describe the gift reads as follows:

"Poverty" as a Malaise of Development

'... you can do your Christmas shopping and help Oxfam to overcome poverty and suffering'

When I read this I felt like laughing and crying at the same time. On the one hand, it's a bright and cheerful way to recapture the importance of donating to charity. On the other hand, it is still encouraging the western consumer to enjoy wasteful consumption. It simply wraps up gift-giving to the poor as part of gift-giving in general. The irony here is that gift-giving is well known (in anthropology) to reflect social differentials and quite often to be a way of showing either patronage or submissiveness. The patron gives gifts to those they wish to patronise; the submissive 'low' ranking person gives gifts to show respect to those above her/him. This well-known pattern is found in many diverse societies. In Japan, the giving of gifts has outlasted the growth of commercialisation. It is very popular and occurs around marriage times, on meeting visitors, within the family, at work, and at some ceremonial events. Oxfam, by using a discourse of gift-giving for requesting charity donations, is clearly suggesting that readers will feel that they are successful patrons if they simply allocate some money to the cause. There is no need for them to pursue issues of administrative efficiency, targeted aid vs. unconditional aid, or how the chosen recipients were chosen. To me the essence of the charity donation discourse is that there is no democratic or public realm where the targets of charity can communicate with the givers of charity. The givers are essentially protected from the realities of struggle over resources. They are beyond criticism.

Poverty: Malaise of Development

The Social Exclusion/Inclusion Discourse

Look now at column two of Tables 1 and 2. Here the social inclusion discourse is described. In wider contexts, such as social and economic policy in Europe, social inclusion is the flip side of what has been called the social exclusion approach to poverty. A bit of history is useful here. Social exclusion is considered normatively wrong because the belonging of citizens is considered sacrosanct across European democracies. Indeed, in some parts of Europe, this 'belonging' is not just a link between the individual and the state, which confers some legal rights to citizens (Byrne, 1999). It is also a sense of shared social solidarity. Thus instead of social inclusion being an act of charity, for many French, or Germans, it is a deeper sense of shared history and values, a sense of solidarity and togetherness. Habermas (1986) describes this as distinct from individualistic concepts of democratic rights. However in Britain (where I live) the social exclusion discourse was taken up as a central plank in Labour's policies before and after their 1997 election victory. For 'New' Labour, social exclusion was a way to describe the ravages of poverty, and social inclusion was a set of policies which not only 'gave to' the poor their rights, but also required from the policy targets a set of behaviours, which Blair and other politicians, called 'their responsibilities' (Fairclough, 2000). Poor people have been redesignated as policy targets. Blair's discourse was studied carefully by Fairclough, and the policies have been studied by many experts (notably Smith and Morton (2006), in relation to employment.

The social inclusion discourse (as found in Britain, both in domestic policy and in international development policy) argues that the poor people have responsibility to act in proper ways, to work hard and train themselves, and

"Poverty" as a Malaise of Development

that in exchange for these decent behaviours, compliant citizens can participate fully in society. An underlying argument is that no matter how low your income, e.g. the minimum wage, you are still an accepted member of society. The 'society' here is the nation-state. Government is an important actor in this discourse. In the EU, this discourse is linked up with the assertion of basic human rights (Milcher and Ivanov, 2008). Ironically, it has been turned into quite an individualistic type of discourse in recent years. The worker's supply of labour is seen as crucial; they must not be lazy or they will become excluded. The latest phrase in the social inclusion discourse is employability. The workers must make themselves highly employable, in which case a labour market will successfully integrate them. All else will follow – decent housing, medical care and pension – if only workers will earn enough money for themselves. This has moved a long way from the original sense of social solidarity that is found in core states of Europe. In this sense in the UK, New Labour discourse has become somewhat neoliberal (individualistic and commercially minded) while other Europeans still hold out for some fundamental unconditional rights and do not blame workers for their own unemployment. In New Labour's social inclusion discourse, the poor are partly to blame for their own poverty, and are agents of their own empowerment. If they persist in being lazy, e.g. in 'the workless household' where both parents get unemployment benefits, then they are beyond help.

This arrangement of powers and capabilities has both advantages and disadvantages. On the one hand it enables individuals and families to consider themselves in charge of their destiny. The UK government has encouraged self-employment among women, for example. Many women have become registered as self-employed childminders, facilitating their own sense of autonomy in work, whilst also supporting the paid work of other mothers who can trust the registered childminder – and must pay them – to mind the kids. Another example of self-autonomy in this discourse is that the government encourages people to take out private health insurance and a private pension to supplement the inadequate state provision. The obvious disadvantage of this system of 'justice' is that it does not promote social equality. Instead, it continuously promotes a growth of inequality in which state provision is for the poor and private provision is for the well off. Basic reasons for poverty, such as having a poor education or lacking experience of employment, are not dealt with. Indeed, the government has no industrial strategy and does not intervene when companies sell out to Indian or other international buyers. Jobs are being moved to other countries, and the state waits for workers to get themselves re-employed. Thus, social inclusion is a theme in politics, but it does not underpin many constructive policies to include people.

The Economic Discourse of Poverty

The third poverty discourse is the one economists often use. The economics of poverty are seen as lying in causal explanations of why people and households are poor, and what it is about the non-poor that makes them different. Numerous famous economists can be cited – Dollar (2001), Dollar and Kraay (2001), Dollar and Gatti (1999), Rama (2003), Ravallion (1998), Ravallion and Datt (1996), for example. These economists hold certain types of theory dear. Firstly, there is the theory that people maximise their utility and try to better themselves, whilst also trading off paid work against more desirable leisure activities.

"Poverty" as a Malaise of Development

Secondly, we have the theory of human capital. In this theory people's earnings reflect their education and acquired skills. Investment in education is seen as rational individual choice, and if wages are low for a group (e.g. for women) then they may not invest in schooling because it won't repay the investment. The higher-response group, e.g. men, may get more investment because it is rational to prefer to invest where returns are higher rather than where returns are stagnant. Thus a mental model of a capital market is used to envision how decisions are made in the schooling market and labour market. Thirdly, the economists usually focus on firms as an important locus of decision making. Firms pay wages, and the tradeoff here is that if they hire more people on lower wages, then poverty may go down, compared with hiring just a few people, in more capital-intensive work, on higher wages. Some economists advocate labour-intensive growth as a way to alleviate poverty. This approach accepts that low-wage work will predominate for the poor. It accepts high levels of economic inequality, while acknowledging that those who lack any paid work at all will suffer from poverty in modern industrialised societies.

All the discourses share a sense that people will be better off if they can be enabled to earn a living and to make themselves better off. Thus at some anodyne level these discourses of poverty converge.

It would be dangerous to attribute too much explanatory power to discourses. Green's paper seems to suggest that discourses create poverty (Green, 2006). Does she mean that discourses of poverty create poverty where before there was none? Her view is probably that the history of poverty is, in part, the history of poverty discourses. But my question about causality may seem a bit confused. There is an underlying philosophical question – does poverty exist prior to its description, when it is encapsulated into a narrative within a discourse? If we answer yes, we presume too much. (This begs the question and essentialises poverty.) If we answer no, then we will inevitably have trouble studying the causes of poverty, because by taking an anti-essentialist position (which feminists call anti-foundationalist) we are making it impossible to study the thing that people are trying to describe.

Through long years of field visits in both UK and India, and close study of texts from anthropology and economics as well as sociology, I have concluded that suffering exists, and that this statement is a better starting point than 'poverty exists' (Amato, 2001). However we can use words about 'poverty' to describe the sources of suffering, since poverty – by its nature, or by what we mean to pin down when we say 'poverty' – implies some suffering. I take a realist view of poverty (Olsen, 2007). That makes me think that discourses of poverty nobly try to get at the problem, and sometimes fail, yet in the meantime are interesting in themselves.

There are many other discourses of poverty – one might for example mention the participation discourse, in which participation in development is thought to potentially reduce poverty; the human needs discourse, which in the 1970s had been called Basic Needs, and so on. I have just described three because I thought that the reader could relate more easily to these.

The next section will discuss two problems that arise in relation to the three poverty discourses; the contradictions they imply for the user of the discourse; and their explanatory weaknesses.

"Poverty" as a Malaise of Development

Dealing with False Discourses

In treating the discourses as if they could be 'false' I am referring to separate work on causality that argues that truth is contested and that knowledge is generally fallible (Olsen and Morgan, 2005; Morgan and Olsen, 2007 and 2008). I feel bound to point out two glaring problems with the discourses listed above. This does not mean they are wholly untrue. Indeed truth and falsehood probably have a large overlap area in social science. But these problems are serious.

i) Performative contradictions of the poverty discourses

Firstly, the speaker who uses the social exclusion/inclusion discourse engages in a contradictory moment, called a 'performative contradiction', by excluding the poor from autonomous action. Just by labelling them poor and making 'them' a them, and 'us' (the experts or the government) an us, the speaker creates a social division that tends to be patronising and disempowering for really poor people. Having a performative contradiction makes it impossible for policies drawn up under this discourse to attack the nerve centres of poverty creation. Instead, the policies are mainly ameliorative. I would go further and argue that ameliorative reforms in capitalism actually help to reproduce poverty and elitism. But this comes from my own position (see conclusion of paper) – instead let's look more closely at an example to illustrate the performative contradiction.

Milcher and Ivanov (2008), define and discuss social inclusion as follows:

Poverty: Malaise of Development

Social inclusion is a relatively new concept promoted especially by the European Union (EU). The EU defines social inclusion as "a process which ensures that those at risk of poverty and social exclusion gain the opportunities and resources necessary to participate fully in economic, social and cultural life and to enjoy a standard of living and well-being that is considered normal in the society in which they live". Thus, social inclusion is understood as both a relative concept where exclusion can only be judged by comparing the circumstances of some individuals (or groups or communities) relative to others ... and as a normative concept which places emphasis on the individual's right of "having a life associated with being a member of a community". In order to achieve these rights, inclusion policies have to address institutional inefficiencies, which derive from exclusionary acts by agents based on power and social attitudes and result in multiple disadvantages based on gender, age, ethnicity, location, economic, education, health status or disability, etc." (p. 1; Milcher and Ivanov did not cite any reference for their quoted phrases.)

A stronger and more concerted rejection of structuralism in favour of individualistic reductionism is hard to imagine. Yet the rejection is subtly framed, taking the form of a positive statement in favour of human rights and against inefficiency. Who could disagree? The net result is that the discourse tends to leave poor people to blame for their position, and responsible for their own rescue. After all, it is they, not the state that create the inefficiency. They are not **in** the state that is so inefficient. The essence of the argument is that they are outside of the state.

The tone of such writings is patronising and state-ist yet, ironically, (and confusingly) at the same time, liberal in the soft, 'small l' sense of being socially progressive. Whilst progressive, such liberal views do not enable the "poor" to get into policy processes. Instead, they patronise poor people and keeps them separate from the well-educated, technocratic classes. (In Salford, where I am politically and socially active, we see this in everyday life.)

"Poverty" as a Malaise of Development

Social inclusion is wishful thinking for those on the top of a heap of inequality.

The Milcher and Ivanov (2008) example also shows some other weaknesses that all three poverty discourses have in common. These weaknesses are ontological, i.e. at the level of deep assumptions about what the world is like. First, the authors in all three discourses assume that markets are a necessary part of the solution to problems. Second, the analyses are all rather individualistic. They do not allow for social solidarity or any profound grounding ethics, except rational choice. Third, patronage is seen to be good, in that it is independent of any analysis of the ethics of inequality. Patronage is missing only from the 'economic discourse of poverty' where it would be considered irrational. This is an important exception and one worth thinking about. The role of patronage and charity, in an anti-poverty ethic, is the subject of interesting current research (Sayer, 2005). In general, serious ethical analysis does not use simplistic discourses like the charity or the social inclusion discourse. See Alkire and Black (1997), Clark (2002), or Habermas (1998) for examples of serious ethical analysis in the context of poverty.

So far, I have suggested that a performative contradiction in the social exclusion discourse makes it seem confused. Other authors have suggested that we need to see poverty more relationally, rather than seeing the poor as a separate group (Green and Hulme, 2005). And one argument is that poverty planning is a political negotiation which should be democratic – a discussion among equals – not a technical or bureaucratic targeting exercise (Hickey and Bracking, 2005). The more conspiracy-theory oriented authors even see social inclusion and other false discourses as a distinctive, deliberate, carefully planned exercise that distracts them while pauperisation goes on and on (Harriss-White, 2006).

Poverty: Malaise of Development

I suggest that when we do study the real causes of suffering through poverty, we must carefully avoid these performative contradictions. Starting from first principles, we construct a realist approach to poverty which accepts the strengths and limitations of each aspect of the complex social world (Martins, 2007). Realists usually tend to think mostly of the aim of human flourishing and then focus on the real structural causes of human poverty/suffering. I am going to turn to this area now, where the other poverty discourses are so weak.

ii) The falsehood of masking the real causal role of social class relations.

Structures of social class are changing all the time. By definition a structure is a set of social locations and the relationships between people in these metaphorical "locations", e.g. worker, elite, business person. Structuralists argue that structures are more than metaphors because they have real effects of two kinds: one, their effect upon the elements in the structures, e.g. being a worker in a job affects the worker. Two, their emergent properties go beyond the nature of the different parts of the structure. For example, class relations evolve as people migrate from villages to cities, but the nature of class relations is not simply the sum of the proportions of people in different types of job, in each place. It also involves larger properties of the whole society, such as inequality and hence the emergence of real poverty. Thus structures have real effects. Structures are also durable. Their enduring – but not permanent – nature makes us tend to call them 'structures' rather than simply norms or institutions. Authors who have set out this ontology

"Poverty" as a Malaise of Development

include Gimenez (1999), Sayer (2005), and Elder-Vass (2007).

The main structures in capitalist societies in the 20th and 21st centuries include ethnic groups, social classes and gender relations. These structures themselves have causal powers so there are powerful mechanisms operating upon both rich and poor people 'from outside themselves'. These causes are not determining, though; there are also some countervailing causes. One's tendency to stay uneducated can be fought by borrowing money to pay for an education. But then one must pay interest on the loan and perhaps do bonded labour to repay it. One may have to drop out of education to repay the loan. So the worker returns to the state of low formal education, even though they have learned some interesting lessons. The worker's agency is exercised to try to fight toward a different position in the class society. Agency is not always successful. Even when it succeeds, it may only move the worker around but not change the class structure itself (Sayer, 1992, chapters 1-3).

My argument, that the three discourses are false, rests upon the premise that each one hides class relations and the class basis of social action. Other arguments could also be adduced – perhaps about gender and ethnicity, or mothering and other topics – but this one is sufficient for me to have grave concerns about the three discourses.

In brief:

The charity discourse portrays us – the well off – as able to ameliorate some poverty without intervening in any fundamental way to change the structure of social relations between poor and non-poor people.

The social exclusion discourse portrays us – the well-intentioned government agencies – as able to target the

Poverty: Malaise of Development

poor for inclusion, without allowing people to engage freely in the discussion about how society should change. (Defining 'freely' in this claim is contestable; see Habermas for the argument that an immigrant or 'outsider' is not free to engage in the debate because the debate automatically excludes them; Habermas, 1998). Example of authors who challenge capitalism on grounds that it makes workers unfree to discuss poverty alleviation include Harriss-White (2006), and Fine (2001). Fine is particularly condemning of the social inclusion discourse.

Finally, turning to the economists' orthodox discourse, it portrays workers as choosing their own level of poverty. For this discourse everything is 'chosen'. Agency is all. There is no role for structure. In recent years newspapers and governments have begun encouraging workers to make themselves more 'employable'. This goes beyond formal education, as in the human capital model (which was hopeless enough for the poor). Now we have to make our c.v. lengthy, acquire office skills such as discipline and timekeeping, and document our new skills in ways recognised by employers, such as getting National Vocational Qualifications no matter how tedious it is to produce the various portfolios and to welcome the inspectors. Inspectors and portfolios, as well as the audit culture of visiting to check files and poke noses, are now commonly found among self-employed, child care experts and health and safety, accreditation workers. All this arises from, and is consistent with, the employability theme in neoliberal thinking. Make yourself worthy of a job!

Some underlying western ontological assumptions help to bolster the three false discourses. These discourses belie the possibility of real positive change. The assumptions include individualistic reductionism,

"Poverty" as a Malaise of Development

oversimplification of the role of government, and nationalistic policy-making. These ontological assumptions – when re-worked – offer areas for a complete overhaul of both social theory and development theory. That is the current project for experts. Meanwhile social forums and development dialogues continue.

The Transformationalist Strategy

As researchers, we have to navigate between discourses, and we are changed (when growing in our understanding) by doing so. For me, this is part of transformationalism. A transformationalist does not just favour change: they foment it. They do not just criticise power; they transform it through practice. They do not just reject a false discourse, they propose alternatives. In Marx and Lenin's work, transformationalism took the form of *praxis*. It also means being able to make reference to events more accurately in a fundamental way than some false discursive orientation. Transformationalism has been described by authors like Mies (1998) or De Angelis (2007) as people struggling within an unequal society to both change that society, and to change the way society is perceived. Foucault and Gordon (1980) are typical. They aim to make it impossible for the society to go on, with the forms of social relation in which poverty has been produced. Here the transformationalists will appear similar to Green (2006) and Hickey and Bracking (2005) - three post-structuralists who are lightly post-development in their orientation. For an explicit treatment of transformation in development, see Brohman (1996), and for a theorisation of it, see Bhaskar (1986, 1998) or Latouche (1993).

Poverty: Malaise of Development

Summary and Conclusion

In this chapter I described three common ways of talking about poverty. The three I chose are prevalent in the United Kingdom today. I was quite critical of them because, although they try to direct our attention to alleviating suffering, they also mask the effects of basic structures like social class. Those who affiliate to these three discourses – the charity discourse, the social inclusion discourse, and an economic discourse – also engage in a performative contradiction, by inhibiting the transformative potential of 'talk' or analysis. In short, these discourses bear falsehoods and play a masking role in society. The alternative is to study causality through history and to work to re-present our analyses in ways that offer real equality (now) in the world polity and thus help all to move from where we are to somewhere that has more flourishing and less suffering. Our destination is likely to be a less capitalist, less class-ridden place so we need theories that focus on class and capital in a transformative way.

References

Alkire, S., & Black, R. (1997). A practical reasoning theory of development ethics: Furthering the capabilities approach. *Journal of International Development, 9* (2), 263-279.

Amato, J. (2001). Politics of suffering, *International Social Sciences Review*, 69 (1&2), 23-30.

"Poverty" as a Malaise of Development

Berg, E. (1981). *Accelerated development in sub-Saharan Africa ("The Berg Report").* Washington, DC: IBRD.

Bhaskar, R. (1986). *Scientific realism and human emancipation.* London: Verso.

Bhaskar, R. (1998). *The possibility of naturalism: A philosophical critique of the contemporary human sciences.* London: Routledge.

Brohman, J. (1996). *Popular development: Rethinking the theory and practice of development.* Oxford: Blackwell.

Byrne, D. (1999). *Social Exclusion.* Buckingham: Open University Press.

Chouliaraki, L., & Fairclough, N. (1999). *Discourse in Late Modernity: Rethinking critical discourse analysis.* Edinburgh: Edinburgh University Press.

Clark, D. (2002). *Visions of development: A study of human values.* Cheltenham: Edward Elgar.

De Angelis, M. (2007). *The beginning of history: Values, struggle and global capital.* London: Pluto Press.

Dollar, D. (2001). *Globalization, inequality, and poverty since 1980.* Washington, DC: IBRD.

Dollar, D., & Kraay, A. (2001). *Growth is good for the poor.* Washington, DC: IBRD.

Dollar, D., & Gatti, R. (1999). *Gender inequality, income, and growth: Are good times good for women?* Washington, DC: IBRD.

Elder-Vass, D. (2007). For emergence: Refining Archer's account of social structure. *Journal for the Theory of Social Behaviour, 37* (1), 25-44.

Engels, F. (1892). *The condition of the working-class in England in 1844.* Trans Florence Kelley Wischnewetzky. London: S. Sonnenschein & Co.

Fairclough, N. (1992). *Discourse and social change.* Cambridge: Polity.

Fairclough, N. (1995). *Critical Discourse Analysis: The critical study of language.* Harlow, England: Longman.

Fairclough, N. (2000). *New Labour, New Language?* London; New York: Routledge.

Fairclough, N. (2001). *Language and Power*, 2nd ed. Harlow: Longman.

Fine, B. (2001). *Social capital versus social theory: Political economy and social science at the turn of the millennium.* London, Routledge.

Foucault, M., & Gordon, C. (1980). *Power/knowledge: Selected interviews and other writings, 1972-1977.* New York: Pantheon Books.

"Poverty" as a Malaise of Development

Gimenez, M. (1999). For structure: A critique of ontological individualism. *Journal of the International Association for Critical Realism* [then called *Alethia*], 2 (2), 19-25.

Green, M. (2002). Social development: Issues and approaches. In U. Kothari & M. Minogue (Eds.), *Development Theory and Practice: Critical Perspectives.* (pp. 52-70). London: Palgrave.

Green, M. (2006). Representing poverty and attacking representations: Perspectives on poverty from social anthropology. *Journal of Development Studies, 42* (7), 1108-1129. (also see an earlier version at Global Poverty Working Group Working Papers Number 9, Retrieved 2007, from: www.gprg.org)

Green, M., & Hulme, D. (2005). From correlates and characteristics to causes: Thinking about poverty from a chronic poverty perspective. *World Development, 31* (3), 867-879.

Habermas, J. (1986). *Autonomy and solidarity.* Interviews. London: Verso.

Habermas, J. (1998, original 1996). *The inclusion of the other. Studies in political theory.* Cambridge: MIT Press.

Harriss-White, B. (2006). Poverty and capitalism. *Economic and Political Weekly, 41* (3), April 1, 2006.

Hickey, S., & Bracking, S. (2005). Exploring the politics of chronic poverty: From representation to a politics of justice? *World Development, 33* (6), 851-865.

Hutchinson, F., Mellor, M., et al. (2002). *The politics of money: Towards sustainability and economic democracy.* London: Pluto Press.

Iyengar, S. (1990). Framing Responsibility for Political Issues: The Case of Poverty. *Political Behaviour, 12* (1), 19-40.

Kinnick, K. N., Krugman, D. M., & Cameron, G. T. (1996). Compassion fatigue: Communication and burnout toward social problems, *Journalism and Mass Communication Quarterly, 73* (3), 687-707.

Langley, P., & Mellor, M. (2002). 'Economy', sustainability, and sites of transformative space. *New Political Economy, 7* (1), 49-66.

Latouche, S. (1993). *In the wake of the affluent society: An exploration of post-development.* London: Zed Press.

Martins, N. (2007). Ethics, Ontology and Capabilities. *Review of Political Economy, 19* (1), 37-53.

Mies, M. (1998). *Patriarchy and accumulation on a world scale: women in the international division of labour.* London: Zed.

"Poverty" as a Malaise of Development

Milcher, S., & Ivanov, A. (2008). Social inclusion and human development, *HDR Networks*, January, 16, p. 1. Retrieved March 2008 from: http://hdr.undp.org/en/hdinsights_jan2008.pdf

Morgan, J., & Olsen, W. (2007). Defining objectivity in realist terms: Objectivity as a second-order "bridging" concept, *Journal of Critical Realism*, 6 (2), see http://www.equinoxjournals.com/ojs/index.php/JCR/

Morgan, J., & Olsen, W. (2008). Objectivity as a second-order "bridging" concept, Part 2: Bridging into action, *Journal of Critical Realism*, 7 (1), see http://www.equinoxjournals.com/ojs/index.php/JCR/

Olsen, W. K., & Morgan, J. (2005). A critical epistemology of analytical statistics: Addressing the sceptical realist. *Journal for the Theory of Social Behaviour, 35* (3), 255-284.

Olsen, W. K. (2007), Poverty, pp. 370-371. In M. Hartwig (Ed.) *Dictionary of Critical Realism*, London: Routledge.

Orwell, G., & Davison, P. H. (2001). *The road to Wigan Pier.* London: Penguin.

Rama, M. (2003). *Globalization and workers in developing countries.* Washington, DC: IBRD.

Ravallion, M. (1998). On reform, food prices and poverty in India. *Economic and Political Weekly, 33* (1-2), 29-36.

Ravallion, M., & Datt, G. (1996). "How important to India's poor is the sectoral composition of economic growth?" *World Bank Economic Review, 10* (1), 1-25.

Roberts, R. (1971). *The classic slum: Salford life in the first quarter of the century.* Manchester: Manchester University Press.

Sayer, A. (1992). *Method in social science.* London: Routledge.

Sayer, A. (2005). *The moral significance of class.* Cambridge: Cambridge University Press.

Skeggs, B. (1997). *Formations of class and gender: Becoming respectable.* London: Sage Publications.

Smith, P., & Morton, G. (2006). Nine years of New Labour: neoliberalism and workers' rights. *British Journal of Industrial Relations, 44* (3): 401-420.

Wark, M. (1995). Fresh maimed babies, *Transition, 65,* 36-47.

Wright, C. (2004). Consuming lives, consuming landscapes: Interpreting advertisements for Cafédirect coffees. *Journal of International Development, 16,* 665-680.

"Poverty" as a Malaise of Development

Yapa, L. (1996). What causes poverty? A postmodern view. *Annals of the Association of American Geographers, 86* (4), 707-728.

CRITICAL PERSPECTIVES ON ISSUES OF GLOBAL POVERTY

Robert Biel

Introduction

Poverty has always been functional to any form of class society, in obliging people to work hard under bad conditions. This is particularly the case where society (as with capitalism) is based on the market rather than on personal servitude. The current form of capitalism simply develops this in a particular way. For example, in the 'new management systems' generalised since 1980, a relatively small number of people experience stable working conditions, surrounded by a mass of others whose status is precarious and informal. The former dare not challenge their conditions for fear of being cast into the outer wilderness, a situation cynically exploited by management (cf. Butz & Leslie, 2001). The North-South divide develops this duality at a global level, with cheap labour, premised on an ambient poverty, being justified as an essential competitive advantage.

For this reason, the notion of 'making poverty history' has no place within the logic of capitalism in general or, more specifically, of its contemporary form. It makes sense as a radical notion, critical of that entire logic; but, as part of the mainstream discourse, it is likely to be merely cosmetic.

Why then, the fixation with poverty within the current development paradigm? Although the notion of eliminating poverty may be merely cosmetic, the need to manage it is a real and burning issue. The usefulness of poverty can never entirely be divorced from its other side:

the spectre of social disorder. It will be helpful to analyse this problem into two aspects: firstly, the relational issue; and secondly, the question of whether there is some deeper significance of poverty as an indicator of the limits, decline or 'entropy' of the mode of production. I will discuss the term entropy in more detail below, but for the moment we can take it as signifying an increasing difficulty in maintaining order.

Conceptual framework on the issue of pauperisation

Let us first consider the relational aspect. The most obvious risk is that people will perceive the link between poverty, on the one hand, and wealth and accumulation, on the other. Official poverty discourses, therefore, function to occupy the terrain of debate and squeeze out such uncomfortable notions. In response, the left-wing position has often tended to emphasise poverty's relational character. Logically, the realities of accumulation make wealth flow to those who already control it; hence, even the most favourable reading of development would tend to weaken working people's relative position (Marx, 1849/1969, pp. 166-7). At a national level, rulers frequently seek to gain consensus around a national drive to expand the 'cake', on the reasoning that all will benefit; in a sense, globalisation merely reiterates this promise at a world level. But, even if we take at face value the premise that the 'cake' is growing and that the working population will derive some absolute improvement from such enlargement, this would be fully compatible with the power of the dominant social group increasing, measured in its relative status (Portes & Walton, 1981).

Against this background, the significance of the current agenda is twofold. On the one hand, the targets posed by the Millennium Development Goals [MDGs] tend

Poverty: Malaise of Development

to divert the debate into Victorian notions of absolute poverty (the quantification of minimum standards for the survival and reproduction of the workforce). On the other, whenever relative poverty becomes inescapable, this is in turn diverted into a non-threatening and antiseptic form. For example, World Bank experts tend to colonise the relative poverty discussion by channelling it towards the measurement of disparities in living standards (e.g. Ravallion, 2003). The climate of ideas can thus incorporate an apparently critical debate – one which, for example, questions the MDG approach for insufficiently targeting relative poverty – so long as it does not stray into the territory of class power.

Perhaps, in order to challenge this restriction, we should actually talk about class rather than about poverty. This is partly true, but this paper will nevertheless argue that poverty should not be reduced to class. To understand this, we should consider the second dimension: poverty as an index of the limits or decadence of capitalism.

We should begin by recognising that, from a humanistic standpoint, freedom from poverty should be considered, like any other human right, to be in some sense absolute and not merely relative. This in turn highlights the puzzling inability of capitalism, which creates more wealth than any other system, to resolve it. Aside from the fact that the realities of accumulation will distribute the wealth to those who already control it (thereby tending to increase disparities), is there some more absolute sense in which the mode of production increasingly causes the impoverishment, or immiseration, of large sectors of the population?

An examination of the work of Marx will be helpful. Marx and Engels provided a striking formulation, to the effect that the bourgeoisie "… is unfit to rule because it is

Issues of Global Poverty

incompetent to assure an existence to its slave within his slavery, because it cannot help letting him sink into such a state, that it has to feed him, instead of being fed by him" (Marx & Engels, 1848/1969, p. 119). I will argue that this concept points towards something which we could call an 'entropy of capitalism', in the sense of highlighting the system's inability to fuel itself in a sustainable way, a tendency to deplete the source of its own order: labour, or human capacity (cf. also Marx 1887/1954, pp. 506-7). However the potential of this concept was unfortunately never fully realised, probably because the discussion became diverted into one about relative class power. It is important to understand why this happened, because it will clarify certain crucial issues for our subsequent argument.

Although, as I believe, an absolute approach to poverty is important (because it raises the issues of human rights and entropy), it is a high-risk endeavour: the problem is that any absolute approach runs the risk of veering into determinism. Concretely, in the early 19th century, Malthus had produced a right-wing deterministic theory, in which poverty was deemed to be caused by objective forces, unalterable by any change of social system, making it pointless to struggle for progress. In response, some forces within the labour movement developed their own left-wing version of determinism, taking as its point of departure a narrow reading of the early Marxian vision of pauperisation. In particular, the 'iron law of wages', developed by Lasalle, stated that wages under capitalism would inevitably be driven down to the bare minimum of subsistence.

Marx rightly considered it important to counter this argument, and in so doing highlighted an issue of great importance; by implication, the 'iron law' idea is actually fatalistic, because it leaves no basis for struggle within

Poverty: Malaise of Development

capitalism. Marx countered this by showing that it is precisely struggle which influences the living conditions of the masses to a significant degree (Marx, 1865/1969). This is why, as Sowell shows, Marx increasingly emphasised the proportional or relative nature of poverty, rather than any absolute definition, pointing out for example that, when the value of consumption goods falls because of increased productivity, it is perfectly possible for a shrinking revenue to purchase an increased amount of means of subsistence (Sowell, 1960, pp. 112-3).

Many aspects of this debate seem astonishingly contemporary; for example, the increasing availability of cheap commodities, which we witness today, is clearly compatible with a decline in the working population's relative class status. And more generally, the emphasis on struggle suggests an important idea (taboo within the mainstream poverty discourse): the best way of improving the situation of the poor would be solidarity with grass-roots movements, rather than agendas from above!

But this still leaves an underlying problem, which is both logical and factual. We are assuming a scenario which is 'win-lose' in terms of the crucial issue of class power but, nevertheless, which is 'win-win' in the sense that the absolute level of both capital and labour may increase. But this latter condition can only be met on the premise of increasing the overall 'cake' from which these payoffs are drawn; in other words, unlimited growth. It is questionable whether this is possible. The most fundamental restriction is ecological; but let us first consider whether or not there is also an inbuilt restriction, internal to the social sphere, expressing the limitations to capitalism's own capacity to regulate its tendency to pauperisation.

Issues of Global Poverty

Scope and limitations of capitalism's ability to regulate pauperisation

If grass-roots struggle is rightly highlighted as the most effective response to pauperisation, it is obvious that this would be the least favoured solution for the ruling order! The latter, therefore, seeks to pre-empt it, by addressing the problem (of the social decay caused by pauperisation) on its own terms. This is precisely the significance of all top-down poverty approaches.

The most obvious instrument is public policy. Many branches of capitalist theory (although today's dominant neoliberal paradigm is comparatively weaker in this respect) recognise that individual decisions aimed at maximising profit can create externalities damaging to the long-term basis of the mode of production. This problem could manifest itself in two ways. The first, predominant during earlier phases which depended on employing vast numbers of workers in industry, is that exploitation in the process of production would be pushed to a point where the reproduction of labour became impossible. The second, which comes to the fore in the contemporary model (with its high degrees of mechanisation in some sectors, and segmented workforce with many semi-informal and semi-employed people), is the perception that a group of disaffected people with no interest in the dominant order (characterised for example as 'the underclass' or 'socially excluded') will adversely affect stability. The state, as personification of the collective capitalist, can step in, attempting to redress these twin threats. In so doing, it fulfils also an ideological function, cultivating its image as an impartial actor, enforcing a class-neutral notion of welfare. Contemporary approaches have evolved on the same terrain, adapting as best they can to new realities, where they are squeezed between an

Poverty: Malaise of Development

increased problem (global processes which exceed the capacities of conventional state regulation) and a reduced capacity to act (neoliberalism's tendency to call into question the whole notion of public policy).

So much for the surface form of regulation, conducted by the obvious action of public policy! I will argue, however, that there also exists a more profound and less apparent process, which might be termed 'deep regulation'. Its characteristic mode of operation consists in moving around, from one sphere to another, the decay, degradation or entropy generated by the mode of production. This can be seen under two main aspects.

The first arises within the social sphere, and refers to the export of degradation, and specifically poverty, to subordinate groups, particularly as a means of diffusing tensions within strategic core economic sectors. This occurs at a number of levels: in the recent regime, for example, poverty is shifted down production chains and onto the informal sector. But this is really only an expression of forces already present, and indeed deeply embedded, within the political economy, gender, and the North-South divide, the latter including a strong 'racial' element. From the gender angle, women serve as a regulation mechanism by being absorbed into the formal sector, or cast out, according to economic fluctuations (Biel, 2003). But what concerns us here is particularly the North-South aspect. The dependency perspective introduced the notion of the export of pauperisation (Amin, 1977). We can develop this concept as follows. There is an aspect of the poverty problem which can be addressed by conventional regulation (i.e. public policy), in the sense that the reduction of poverty appears as a 'win-win' scenario for capitalism, because it generates demand. This formed the basis for the social contracts which underpinned the 'high mass consumption' approach initiated by Keynesianism.

Issues of Global Poverty

But the poverty which seems to be removed is, at the deepest level, merely exported to the periphery, as a kind of counterpart to the high-consumption regime at the core. This export (part of the unconventional, 'deep', form of regulation) clearly only postpones the crunch, inasmuch as the limits become those of Southern societies' capacity to absorb the poverty – limits which may be starkly exposed, for example, when gender and core-periphery aspects come together, as in the status of women in the South.

The concrete relevance of this perspective can be illustrated by revisiting part of our earlier argument; the increasing availability of cheap commodities means that the relative status of the working population can fall, even as it receives more goods. This was supposed to happen because of improved productivity. But in today's situation, the cheap goods are primarily supplied by the working population of the South. In this sense, pauperisation is not eliminated, but merely shifted around. Poverty thus has an absolute dimension (in the sense of an entropic 'arrow of time') which, arguably, we can only properly perceive from an anti-Eurocentric and gender-aware perspective.

The second issue is the export of social problems onto the physical environment. The easiest way to regulate the destructive effects of poverty would be to expand the total size of the cake, leaving relational aspects unchanged, but removing absolute poverty. Of course, enlarging the cake does not in itself guarantee such a result, because the powerful elements could use their power to appropriate the whole of the increment, but at a discourse level it provides a strong argument. The old modernisation theory claimed to have discovered the secret of such 'self-sustained growth', and it is hard to deny that the cake-enlarging claims of the current globalisation discourse (for all its supposed critique of modernisation), are effectively the same. But the cake does not really grow from itself; it always depends on the physical environment, and poses the question of degrading the latter's carrying capacity. Rapid ecological degradation over recent decades is thus, in an important sense, an expression of the 'export of poverty'. For example, attempts have been made to defuse what has historically been the main symptom of poverty (i.e. hunger), but at the expense of undermining the long-term structure of the soil, farming animals in a manner which encourages massive health hazards or manipulating genes with unpredictable results. Or, 'efficiency' savings, from a totally specialised global economy (which eliminates local self-reliance), are achieved by a massive increase in transportation, depleting non-renewable resources and contributing to global warming. In both cases, the respite gained by exporting the social problem onto the physical environment is obviously only temporary – there will be a blowback and, once this occurs, the entropy will come home to roost in the social sphere. Although we cannot develop the environmental dimension within the scope of the current chapter (for further discussion, see Biel, 2006), it must be considered to underlie all the issues to do with poverty and to circumscribe any approaches to solving it.

It therefore seems that the room to manoeuvre is shrinking. In order to understand this more concretely, let us now consider the relationship between poverty and development.

Poverty in relation to the notion of development

Within ruling discourses, the main answer to the North-South dimension of poverty has generally been 'development'. Following our earlier categorisation, it may be helpful to distinguish development into three

Issues of Global Poverty

aspects: the ideology (myth); the sphere of public policy, which seeks to address social reality (different from the myth) and regulate those effects of poverty which are harmful to capitalism's stability; and finally, a 'deep' dimension, the real changes in the political economy which may be very different from what policy is trying to achieve.

The key to modernisation's perception of the poverty issue was its attitude to the thing which development aims to escape from: i.e. the pre-developmental situation (or 'traditional society'). This notion confused two very different phenomena: firstly, the poverty sometimes caused by traditional class exploitation, which caused starving peasantries sporadically to rebel against their rulers; and secondly, sufficiency: the sense in which traditional societies produced what they consumed, had very little use for money at the local level, and had leisure time because there was no incentive to accumulate. The first of these things would obviously be useful to get rid of, but the second is actually something good: from an ecological point of view, if humanity is to have a future, it will need to rediscover sufficiency (cf., for example, Gorz, 1992). But the modernisers lumped both together as the enemy of progress: the situation in which people drew high levels of welfare from their land and natural resources was condemned (for example, by Rostow, 1960, p. 277); and Lewis (1958) was horrified by the 'idleness' (i.e. leisure) witnessed in traditional rural society.

At the 'deep', or tertiary, level we could argue that development, in a certain sense, becomes the liquidation of the non-monetary, non-commodity sphere. This was begun by modernisation and carried through even more intensively by the current paradigm. This is the strongest element of continuity.

Poverty: Malaise of Development

At the ideological level, though, modernisation differed in important respects from its successor. It espoused a 'stages' perspective, whereby the claim to be eliminating poverty appears perfectly consistent with an actual increase in poverty in the short term; it is merely a concomitant of the concentration of wealth, indispensable to create a bright industrial future. The modernisers were perfectly up front about this (for example, Lewis, 1955, p. 182). In a context in which the general climate of economics was demand-led, it made sense to argue that inequality, after rising in the early, high-accumulation stage, would necessarily fall, in order to permit the transition to the stage of mass consumption (this is the inverted 'U' represented in the developmental trajectory known as the Kuznets curve).

The problem was that public policy regulation has to deal with the real world, and should therefore not be misled by the myth. Poverty was indeed increasing, but not for the reasons alleged. In reality, the bad side of tradition, the poverty caused by feudal exploitation, was not eliminated and may well have been intensified while, at the same time, a new urban form became increasingly prevalent, driven, not by the 'pull' factor of increasing formal employment, but rather by a 'push' factor of a mixed feudal-capitalist intensified rural exploitation (cf. Baran, 1957/1973). Moreover, mechanisms developed whereby the existing distribution of power was reproduced through the process of development itself. The symptoms were identified quite early by the radicals; for example, that the rich can access credit and start businesses while the poor cannot (Griffin, 1978).

The establishment dare not leave the field clear to the radicals by adhering to the myths of its own discourse, but must, on the contrary, itself operate on the terrain of these real processes, regulating their socially destabilising effects. This is the significance of the change through which the World Bank began to acquire a central development role in the 1970s. Trickle down was no longer respectable, and poverty had to be addressed in the here and now. But this is where the 'deep' level really asserts itself. A new long cycle of the international political economy [IPE] took over, around 1980, and the accumulation logic began to mould everything into its own image, completely subsuming the regulation tools which were supposed to be mitigating its ill-effects. The claim to address poverty as an immediate issue survives, but in an uneasy relationship with its bedfellow, unbridled commoditisation.

The neoliberal response and its contradictions

At the ideological level, the new orthodoxy is inherently less plausible than modernisation, insofar as, with the collapse of demand-side economics, there is no longer a convincing economic rationale for removing poverty. Reaganomics frankly transfers wealth to the wealthy as an incentive for entrepreneurship, and although this is not expressed so bluntly at a global level, it is hard to deny that the globalisation discourse effectively proposes the same thing. If the motivation for eliminating poverty is merely one of charity, this in turn sits uneasily with liberalism's glorification of self-interested profit-seeking as its central principle. And with the abandonment of stages theory, it is no longer possible to rationalise away any current increase of poverty.

Despite this shaky ideological dimension, at the level of practical regulation (the management of poverty) the present system is, in some respects, undoubtedly efficient. If the limits of global capitalism are, in a significant sense, those of the periphery's ability to absorb pauperisation,

Poverty: Malaise of Development

and if those limits are essentially structural, then the key challenge is to use the anti-poverty agenda as a tool of social engineering. Although, at a global level, no one challenges the fact that wealth is channelled to the wealthy, when this tendency occurs at a local level within Southern societies (manifested, for example, in the feedback mechanisms highlighted by the radicals like Griffin (1978), whereby access to credit serves to embed poverty), it would be important to restrict it, at least to the extent of preventing the collapse of those societies upon which the global accumulation process ultimately rests. A key contribution to the 'shallow' regulation of this problem has been the ideas about microcredit, in particular the theorisation of De Soto (2000). Credit is made available to the poor, rather than to the already wealthy, enabling them to set up small businesses to service global production chains and to supply their own infrastructure, such as self-build housing. These developments in turn form part of a major qualitative change in the organisation of capitalism, modelled upon the industrial management systems; networks will exist in society anyway, so the point is to embrace this fact and channel them in a direction helpful to capital accumulation. You will thereby avoid expending the effort on organising everything, achieve low-cost social provision (empowerment is inherently cheaper than the large-budget social engineering of the 1970s World Bank model!) and, perhaps most importantly, prevent the networks developing in more spontaneous, unpredictable, and potentially radical directions.

These achievements of the neoliberal phase are, nevertheless, undermined at the 'deep' development level. Let us consider more closely the entropic dimension which asserts itself at this level.

The notion of fuelling development by liquidating tradition (sufficiency, non-monetary relations) implies a

Issues of Global Poverty

one-off, unrepeatable mobilisation of factors, leaving unanswered the question of where development would go once they were exhausted. Even within the economics establishment, Krugman (1994) recognised this problem. But the radical perspective, represented particularly by Rosa Luxemburg (1913), had already placed this problem within a broader historical, and most importantly global, context. The capitalist core developed through commoditising its own traditional sector, and was able to continue developing by doing the same thing internationally, initially through colonialism. The liquidation of tradition in the South, still very incomplete at the end of World War II, was then massively stepped up through modernisation; but the question remained, 'What next?' The response was globalisation, beginning in the 1980s, which unfolded a much more all-encompassing commoditisation than anything earlier phases of capitalism had imagined. But the 'what next?' question still lingers on, becoming increasingly difficult to answer.

Concretely, the main contradiction is that the shallow regulatory level of development – whatever its temporary successes – is both undermined and usurped by the deeper logic of accumulation, expressed in commoditisation. Continuing where modernisation left off, once urbanisation has become irreversible, the next stage is to liquidate the commons, the common-pool free resources which used to provide the basis for a sufficient, non-commodity economy (for example, water, seed, or previously communally-provided services). This has occurred in two phases, first through structural adjustment, then through the WTO agenda, including the intellectual property issue [Trade Related Intellectual Property, TRIPS] and trade in services [General Agreement on Trade in Services, GATS]. In effect, the anti-poverty agenda has become enslaved to this dominant attractor.

Poverty: Malaise of Development

Microcredit explicitly aims to help people transform their assets into capital, or rather debt, thereby drawing them increasingly into the monetary economy. At the same time, the commoditisation of everything creates an important 'squeeze': incomes would not only have to rise by the increment necessary to raise living standards above the 'poverty line' (however defined); but also by a supplementary amount to cover the increasing need to purchase previously free goods. This fundamental problem has never received sufficient attention. Globalisation therefore takes away with one hand what it claims to give with the other.

So, what kind of society will this produce? There is an interesting duality in the concept of entropy. On the one hand, conventionally regarded as a descent into disorder, it conjures a scenario which has always worried the establishment: chaos among some marginalised stratum, the last resting place of all the disorder purged from elsewhere in the system and exported down the chain until there is nowhere further for it to go. The contradictory opposite of this is the characterisation of entropy in some of the literature (e.g. Swanson, Bailey & Miller, 1997), as equilibrium. From this angle, the system is losing the variety and differentiation which constitute its vitality. We could link this with the process Goonatilake (1982) calls 'hegemonic cultural blanketing'. As it burns up its fuel (the non-commodity economy), capitalism approaches greater homogenisation (through globalisation) and, in parallel, the accentuation of a stifling, as opposed to a creative, form of social differentiation, i.e. inequality. Despite this, a real differentiation and vitality continue to renew themselves within grass-roots initiatives, but increasingly outside the pale of the homogenised order. Interestingly, the cybernetics approach offers a particular take on the social science concept of 'anomie':

disintegration into components, a lack of conventions and shared perceptions (Krippendorff, 1986). While this signifies a certain absence of structure (which looks like disorder), there is another side of anomie in which, as social entropy increases, people become less subject to a hierarchy of control, the latter becoming increasingly alienated from dominant norms (Spencer, 2001). It looks as though this could easily tip over into subversive social movements, suggesting a link with the ideas of Gramsci (1927-33/1971): social movements are shaped by a hegemonic attractor, but under certain conditions might escape it.

The neoliberal development experiment may, therefore, be of limited scope. It will be interesting to consider a possibility that the experiment is undermined by a kind of export of entropy into the sphere of governance itself, in the sense that the latter just becomes too complex to fulfil its tasks – including the suppression or co-optation of spontaneous grass-roots emergence. As part of the paradigm shift, capitalism has, to some extent, progressed beyond simple state-level public policy, evolving a form of regulation premised upon complexity and pluralism. But this adaptation faces extraordinary challenges, which may well overwhelm it. The complexity of the problems to be regulated constantly increases: for example, the relatively simple relationship between poverty, labour in manufacturing industry and demand has been replaced by one in which poverty is primarily focused in a large marginalised segment, not functional in terms of either consumption or production (although still indirectly functional in the sense that their impoverished conditions serve as a constant reminder to the employed of the fate which awaits them if they rebel). Negative externalities are increasingly focused at a global level, without any equivalent of the state to redress them. But

Poverty: Malaise of Development

above all, the governance sphere witnesses a problem similar to the one we have already identified more generally: the means of regulation are captured by the problem they are supposed to regulate! The whole 'new public management' strategy thus largely involves copying corporate policies (translating them into the public sphere), rather than creating an external force to regulate them. It is no surprise, then, that when the call for the creation of an international level of public policy surfaces within mainstream debates (e.g. Reinicke, 1997), it largely signifies the facilitation of corporate governance, rather than any attempt to restrict it.

The alienation of the homogenised world order from social reality is more than anything expressed in globalisation's war against local, self-reliant economies; exactly the thing the poor need to shield them from the shocks which would arise if, as is likely, the global system becomes dislocated. And even the charitable discourse (which, in the absence of an economic rationale for removing poverty, effectively dominates the aid agenda) can easily get subsumed by the same logic. This was illustrated in a striking way by the Live 8 music event held in 2005, which hitched itself to the most extreme neoliberal discourse. Effectively, the argument was that Africa is being held down by the selfish actions of some backwoodsmen who resist the inevitable march of market fundamentalism, such as the proponents of small-scale agriculture and food self-sufficiency in Europe; if these reactionaries are swept out of the way, the argument goes, Africa can enter a brave new world in which it converts its land and economy entirely to providing cheap agricultural goods for external consumers. This scenario would undoubtedly benefit a certain group of capitalists in the core, who are short-sightedly fixated on the general increase of the rate of profit which would result from a

Issues of Global Poverty

reduction in the European cost of living, owing to cheaper food. But it would undercut the regulation aspect of capitalism, its need to limit the social entropy which follows the alienation of accentuated market fundamentalism.

According to our hypothesis, that the increasing difficulty of maintaining social structure would be reflected in the sphere of governance, we would expect an important focus to be the position of Southern elites.

Their status with respect to the dominant poverty agenda is ambiguous. In one respect, they have discovered a niche, notably in the generation of discourses. Here, we find a self-reinforcing systemic mechanism of collective denial, orchestrated by the World Bank. As an advocate of social engineering, a stance which pits it against the anti-interventionist US neoconservatics, the Bank has no interest in downplaying the extent of poverty. But there is a dilemma. Whereas the old 'stages' theorists would have no problem in rationalising a current increase in poverty, in today's climate the statistics must show globalisation tending to reduce poverty immediately. It is not difficult to obtain this result. The technical issues in poverty-measurement are sufficiently complex for governments to have immense scope to manipulate the figures to show a favourable trend, which they have always done at a single country level (cf., for example, Macarov, 2003). But now this becomes part of a global dynamic: the Bank hands Southern states a responsibility, via Poverty Reduction Strategy Papers [PRSPs] to demonstrate 'pro-poor' growth, elites respond by massaging the statistics, and the Bank then adds up these country-level statistics to show that poverty is shrinking at a global level![1] This continues to

---

[1] Even then, the figures are only made to add up by an extraordinary distortion of the significance of the Chinese data. In reality, China's

Poverty: Malaise of Development

require ongoing statistical massaging: in 2008 (Ravallion et al. 2008), in a major revision, the World Bank admitted that there were 400 million more extremely poor people who had failed to appear in previous estimates; but since the document also revised the previous figures, the trend in reducing poverty was made to appear the same. In the 2009 World Development Report (World Bank 2009), inequality is conveniently reduced to disparities between countries and regions, thus creating a supplementary argument in favour of free trade!

But for all this co-operative statistical ballet, at the more substantive level of the development which is really taking place, the elites are in a more difficult position. The two great questions of capitalist development remain what they have always been: can the South draw some benefit from the global economy?; and if so, can the developmental effects be somehow embedded within society? Globalisation certainly opens a possibility for responding in a pragmatic way, to maximise the opportunities while they are there. This is an interesting and complex problem, with many pitfalls, but undoubtedly some openings (cf., for example, Kaplinsky, 2005), which can only be answered in the concrete. The problem, however, is that, alongside whatever opportunities are hypothetically created by the

---

earlier Maoist policies (which could scarcely be presented as a vindication of neo-liberalism) created the basis of economic development, while also artificially inflating the amount of poverty, because most services were provided by the collective with relatively little need for money. With China's subsequent adaptation to globalisation, although in real terms the destruction of the collective may often render living conditions more difficult, the influx of wealth creates the illusion of a phenomenal reduction of the poverty at a national, and therefore (because of the size of China's population) global level, while simultaneously the North-South differential also appears to decrease.

global value chain, there is also a kind of 'entropy chain' whereby anomie is shifted to the South. It is hard to escape a sense that the Northern rulers (who accept no equivalent responsibility for redistribution within their own countries, still less at a global level) are offloading onto Southern elites the responsibility – even the guilt! – for social entropy and saddling them with the task of its governance. The confusion, and ambiguity, of the perceptions of the elites, revealed in some empirical studies (e.g. Reis & Moore, 2005), their strong perception of poverty as 'agent of chaos', is only too explicable in this context. Managerial slogans like decentralisation and subsidiarity appear merely as euphemisms for a process whereby those at the top of the food chain of international exploitation insulate themselves from the worst effects of the disorder it generates.

The 'normal' mode of governance is thus placed under increasingly severe strain. And this is where the 'war on terror' comes into the picture, to pick up the pieces.

It is sometimes assumed that the 'war on terror' is an external distraction to the anti-poverty agenda, but in reality the two are intimately related. The poverty situation always involves an endemic violence, and the war on terror's fundamental premise is to delegitimise anyone who is on the 'underside' of a violent social relationship. For this purpose, it has created an international arsenal of repressive measures. The most obvious are military measures to proscribe any organised grass-roots responses to the violence of poverty, or to invade countries in which grass-roots campaigns hook up with a new definition of state power, in order to question the global order. But there is also direct intervention in the development field. For example, the current agenda operates on the terrain of networks, but is very distrustful of any parallel ones. New measures therefore become

Poverty: Malaise of Development

available (under the excuse of combating the funding of 'terrorism') to clamp down on alternative financial channels, whereby migrant workers from the South might seek to channel remittances in such a way as to escape the dominant development project.

In this sense, the anti-poverty discourse and the 'war on terror' are two sides of the same coin; the former stipulating the safe limits within which poverty issues can be addressed, and the latter repressing individuals or groups adjudged to have transgressed these.

But, ultimately, they are contradictory. This explains the historic, almost Shakespearian, duality of Tony Blair, the sense of (probably tragic) destiny which clung to him as he attempted to pursue in parallel the two strands. The development paradigm operates in an indirect and subtle way on a terrain of political pluralism and civil society. It seeks to embrace emergent and spontaneous social phenomena, such as networks, and channel them in acceptable directions. But, at a certain point, a controlled network society becomes a contradiction in terms! It is inherently vulnerable to the development of autonomous networks or to rival attractors, emerging to draw them away from the dominant paradigm. Movements of the poor themselves are necessarily problematic to the dominant interests. There may be a checklist to identify those who develop anti-systemic traits but, if they proliferate too much (as seems likely, in Latin America for example), this will become impossibly complex to enforce. The local state may have been weakened too much to repress them effectively, or may even negotiate a compromise with them. Even a relatively minor global crisis could trigger a positive feedback loop, with unpredictable consequences; the logical defence for the poor is a return to sufficiency (whether at a community, national or South-South level). This would be a response to a weakening of the global economy, but would also function as a cause of a further such weakening.

For all these reasons, the two aspects – the development/poverty agenda and the militaristic one – although apparently complementary, are not really in a stable equilibrium. They only appear to be in equilibrium at this precise juncture, because they meet while travelling in opposite directions. The rise of repression and militarism ultimately signifies an admission of defeat for the 'soft' (developmental) response to poverty.

Conclusion

We have seen that a radical reading of the relative poverty issue highlights the fact that struggle from below (by the poor themselves) is the most effective way of limiting poverty. In order to prevent this, dominant interests try to fill all ideological space with their own discourses about the causes of poverty (although this is hardly addressed today) and solutions to it. At the same time, these discourses have to deliver, not necessarily what they claim to deliver – the abolition of poverty – but the regulation of its destabilising effects. But for several reasons, most noticeably a growing complexity and the powerful objective tendency of globalisation to capture even the approaches supposed to regulate it, this is increasingly a losing battle. Hence the issue of the degree of poverty – ultimately a reflection of the rate of exploitation – will continue to be determined by struggle.

While thus affirming the importance of the relative poverty issue, this chapter also argues that a certain 'absolute' dimension remains essential. A critique of deterministic approaches (which would tend to downgrade the role of struggle) is fully compatible with recognition of a certain entropic tendency, whereby

Poverty: Malaise of Development

capitalism increasingly degrades both its social and ecological basis. There is a real sense of the degradation being exported 'down the chain', and at a certain point the issue is posed that there is nowhere further to export it. Most notably, there is the fundamental theme of commoditisation, and much of what passes itself off as poverty-alleviation can easily be revealed as commoditisation in disguise. This has potentially devastating implications for those on low incomes. It is precisely this entropic dimension which defines the background against which the theme of struggle will unfold.

References

Amin, S. (1977). *La loi de la valeur et le matérialisme historique.* Paris: Editions de Minuit.

Baran, P. A. (1973). *The political economy of growth.* Harmondsworth: Penguin. (Original ed. published 1957).

Biel, R. (2003). Le capitalisme a besoin des femmes. In J. Bisilliat (Ed.), *Regards de femmes sur la globalisation* (pp. 28-34). Paris: Karthala.

Biel, R. (2006). The interplay between social and environmental degradation in the development of the international political economy. *Journal of World-Systems Research, 12* (1), 109-47.

Butz, D., & Leslie D. (2001). Risky subjects: Changing geographies of employment in the automobile industry. *Area, 33* (2), 212-9.

Goonatilake, S. (1982). *Crippled minds: An exploration into colonial culture.* New Delhi: Vikas.

Gorz, A. (1992). L'écologie politique entre expertocratie et autolimitation. *Actuel Marx, 12,* 15-29.

Gramsci, A. (1971). *Selections from the prison notebooks of Antonio Gramsci.* (Q. Hoare & G. N. Smith, Eds. & Trans.). London: Lawrence & Wishart. (Originally written 1927-33).

Griffin, K. (1978). *International inequality and national poverty.* London: Macmillan.

Kaplinsky, R. (2005). *Globalization, poverty and inequality: Between a rock and a hard place.* Cambridge: Polity Press.

Krippendorff, K. (1986). Social entropy. In Principia Cybernetica Web, *Web dictionary of cybernetics and systems.* Retrieved February 2006, from: http://pespmc1.vub.ac.be/ASC/SOCIAL_ENTRO.html

Krugman, P. (1994). The myth of Asia's miracle. *Foreign Affairs, 73* (6), 62-78.

Poverty: Malaise of Development

Lewis, W. A. (1955). *The theory of economic growth*. London: Allen & Unwin.

Lewis, W. A. (1958). Economic development with unlimited supplies of labour. In A. N. Agarwala & S. P. Singh (Eds.), *The economics of underdevelopment*. Bombay: Oxford University Press.

Luxemburg, R. (1913). *Die Akkumulation des Kapitals: Ein Beitrag zur ökonomischen Erklärung des Imperialismus*. Berlin: Paul Singer.

Macarov, D. (2003). *What the market does to people: Privatization, globalization and poverty*. Atlanta, GA: Clarity Press.

Marx, K. (1969). Manifesto of the Communist Party. In K. Marx & F. Engels, *Selected works, vol. I*. Moscow: Progress Publishers. (Original work published 1848).

Marx, K. (1969). Wage-labour and capital. In K. Marx & F. Engels, *Selected works, vol. I*. Moscow: Progress Publishers. (Original work published 1849).

Marx, K. (1969). Wages, price and profit. In K. Marx & F. Engels, *Selected works, vol. II*. Moscow: Progress Publishers. (Original work published 1865).

Marx, K., (1954). *Capital, vol. I.* Moscow: Foreign Languages Publishing House. (Original work published 1887).

Portes, A., & Walton J. (1981). *Labor, class and the international system.* New York: Academic Press.

Ravallion, M. (2003). *The debate on globalization, poverty and inequality: Why measurement matters.* Washington DC: World Bank, Development Research Group, Poverty Team.

Ravallion, M., Chen, S., & Sangraula, P. (2008). *Dollar a day revisited,* Policy Research Working Paper No. 4620. World Bank, Development Research Group, Director's office.

Reinicke, W. H. (1997). Global public policy. *Foreign Affairs,* 76 (6), 127-38.

Reis, E. P., & Moore, M. (Eds.). (2005). *Elite perceptions of poverty and inequality.* London: ZED Books.

Rostow, W. W. (1960). *The process of economic growth* (2nd ed.). Oxford: Clarendon Press. (Original ed. published 1952).

Soto, H. de, (2000). *The mystery of capital: Why capitalism triumphs in the West and fails everywhere else.* New York: Basic Books.

Sowell, T., (1960). Marx's 'increasing misery' doctrine. *American Economic Review, 50* (1), 111-20.

Spencer, N. (2001). The network propositions. In N. Spencer, *Prediction science*. Retrieved February 2006, from:

http://www.normanspencer.co.nz/PsNetwork/Propositions.html

Swanson, G. A., Bailey, K. D., & Miller, J. G. (1997). Entropy, social entropy and money: A living systems theory perspective. *Systems Research and Behavioral Science, 14* (1), 45-65.

World Bank (2009). *World Development Report 2009: Reshaping Economic Geography*. Washington, DC: World Bank.

CHILD POVERTY IN A DEVELOPING WORLD[1]

Shailen Nandy

Introduction

Children are often hardest hit by poverty: it causes lifelong damage to their minds and bodies. They are therefore likely to pass poverty on to their children, perpetuating the poverty cycle. Poverty reduction must begin with children (UNICEF, 2000, p. 1)

This paper addresses the issue of child poverty. Interest in the topic has grown in recent years, as governments in both rich and poor countries are confronted with the fact that rates of child poverty are both unacceptably high and growing. Children are now the largest single group living in poverty in many countries (Spencer, 2003), and the latest data from the Department for Work and Pensions shows the UK government has failed to meet its own targets of reducing child poverty (Brewer, Goodman, Shaw & Sibieta, 2006).

There are many reasons why we should be concerned with child poverty. The most obvious would be moral ones, for the suffering of those unable to fend or provide for themselves should be avoided wherever possible. Children depend on adults (be it their families or the state), not least for their survival and care. Moral reasons are

---

[1] I thank colleagues at the University of Bristol for their help, particularly Professor David Gordon, Christina Pantazis, Dr Michelle Kelly-Irving and Dr Simon Pemberton. I would also like to acknowledge the generous support of Professor Peter Townsend who sadly died in June 2009.

supported and reinforced by national and international legislation, designed to protect children's interests and ensure their development (e.g. the 1948 Universal Declaration of Human Rights, the 1989 United Nations Convention on the Rights of the Child). More pragmatic reasons would include the economic "value" of children (as labour, as support in old age), since they often constitute a considerable proportion of the population. Poverty impacts on their social, physical and cognitive development and that in turn can limit their productivity and potential and so prevent their escape from poverty. In extreme cases, poverty can create and contribute to conditions that lead to civil and social breakdown, and eventually to armed conflict or civil war (Carlton-Ford, Hamill & Houston, 2000; Garfield, 2001; Lomo & Hovil, 2004).

This chapter begins with a look at how poverty impacts on the health and development of children. It traces how international concerns about child well-being have evolved over the last century to emerge with a focus on children's rights. The measurement of child poverty in developing countries by researchers at the University of Bristol is discussed, as are the main results. Finally, a short overview of child poverty in rich countries is provided and the chapter concludes with a discussion and summary of the issues that have been raised.

Impact of poverty on children

Poverty damages the lives and well-being of children, irrespective of where they live. While the differences in child health and mortality between rich and poor countries are more noticeable (e.g. through comparisons between rates of infant and child mortality, patterns of morbidity, etc.), differences between rich and poor within countries

Child Poverty in a Developing World

may appear less stark, but are equally important A number of studies show clear socio-economic disparities in child mortality and morbidity in rich countries (Townsend & Davidson, 1988; Whitehead, 1988; Reading, Jarvis & Openshaw, 1993; Adekoga, 1994; Marmot & Feeney, 1997; Roberts, 1997; Wood, 2000; Bennett & Eisenstein, 2001; Davey Smith, 2003; Spencer, 2003). The same disparities between rich and poor exist to an even greater degree in poor countries with a high dependence on agriculture, where rural areas are often the poorest and most underserved by health services (Wang, 2003). The extreme poverty and deprived conditions experienced by inhabitants of the slums, shanty towns and favelas of many cities in developing countries mean their health and mortality rates are often worse than those in rural areas, as they have to contend with overcrowding, environmental pollution, road traffic and violence (World Health Organization [WHO], 1988; Husein, Khan, Omar & Lobo, 1995; Satterthwaite, et al., 1996; Bartlett, Hart, Satterthwaite, De La Barra & Missair, 1999; Haddad, Ruel & Garrett, 1999; Masmas, et al., 2004). The undeniable impact of poverty on people's lives led the WHO to state in the opening of its 1995 World Health Report:

> The world's biggest killer and greatest cause of ill health and suffering across the globe is listed almost at the end of the International Classification of Diseases. It is given code Z59.5 – extreme poverty (WHO, 1995, p. 1.)

An estimated ten to twelve million children die *each year* mostly from preventable causes (Black, Morris & Bryce, 2003). Almost all these deaths occur in poor countries, where poverty is the primary determinant for children not having sufficient food, ready access to health services and medical treatment, or living conditions conducive to growing up safe and healthy. Poverty accounts for why children are not sent to school and why, instead, many millions work long hours in dangerous conditions to help support their families (Siwal, 1980; Woolf, 2002; Strulik, 2004). Many of these children are effectively denied an education by the constraints poverty imposes on them. In many instances, the quality of services (be they education or health) available in poor neighbourhoods are themselves poor and under-resourced, resulting in early drop-out or delayed progression (Mehrotra & Jarrett, 2002). Such differences in the quality of services available to different socio-economic groups are not limited to poor countries, and there is ample evidence of similar patterns in rich countries (Rice, 1991; Blendon et al., 2002). Such discrepancies help determine different outcomes between the rich and poor.

In recent years, international concerns about poverty have led to an increase in interest in the issues of debt, aid, human rights and the role of international financial institutions like the World Bank. Events like Jubilee 2000 and the Make Poverty History campaign show how people around the world are genuinely concerned with the issue of poverty, but it must be noted that similar campaigns launched in the past have rarely been sustained. International interest in the poverty and the well-being of children is nothing new, as the next section demonstrates.

International concerns about child poverty

International concerns about conditions for children have a long history. Following the First World War, Eglantyne Jebb (founder of the Save the Children Fund) and others were instrumental in drawing up the 1924 League of Nations' Declaration of the Rights of the Child. The

Child Poverty in a Developing World

Declaration signalled its concern for the well-being of children by stating that "Mankind owes to the child the best it has to give" and called for the child to "be given the means requisite for its normal development, both materially and spiritually".

The 1959 United Nations Declaration on the Rights of the Child echoed the sentiments of the 1924 Declaration, and established a set of rights, many of which related directly to child welfare. They included rights to adequate nutrition and medical care, to special care if handicapped, and to be among the first to receive relief in times of disaster. Principle 4 went so far as to state:

> The child shall enjoy the benefits of social security. He shall be entitled to grow and develop in health; to this end, special care and protection shall be provided to both him and to his mother, including adequate pre-natal and post-natal care. The child shall have the right to adequate nutrition, housing, recreation and medical services.

The role of the state in providing financial and other assistance for children was stated in Principle 6:

> Society and the public authorities shall have the duty to extend particular care to children without a family and to those without adequate means of support. Payment of State and other assistance towards the maintenance of children of large families is desirable.

Regarding education, Principle 7 stated:

> The child is entitled to receive education, which shall be free and compulsory, at least in the elementary stages.

Poverty: Malaise of Development

However, international interest in the specific rights and needs of children was not sustained in the years following the 1959 Declaration. In an effort to rekindle international interest, the United Nations declared 1979 the International Year of the Child [IYC]. As with all such events, there was an initial surge in enthusiasm and interest, with "many descriptive and analytical exercises undertaken at the national level, intended to identify needs, to create awareness, and to mobilize people around the idea of attention to the 'whole child'" (Myers, 1992, p. 19).

A decade later, these efforts culminated in the 1989 United Nations Convention on the Rights of the Child [UNCRC], which placed the issue of children's rights at the centre of the international stage. The 1989 UNCRC is one of the most important documents concerning the well-being of children and it builds on the foundations provided by the declarations of 1924 and 1959. It sets out clearly the social, economic, civil and political rights to which children *in their own right* are entitled, under four broad categories: survival, development, protection and participation (United Nations, 1989). Importantly, the convention is binding on governments.

Under the UNCRC, and incorporated under the right to survival, are the right to life and the right to adequate living conditions and health services; rights to development include the rights to education, to information, to play and to leisure; rights relating to protection include the right to protection against trafficking and exploitation (either sexual or from harsh working conditions). Lastly, rights relating to participation incorporate the rights of children to have their views and interests represented.

The UNCRC is explicit on a number of rights that, if fulfilled, could have a considerable impact in reducing child poverty:

- Article 4 obliges States Parties "to undertake [such] measures to the maximum extent of their available resources";
- Article 27 sets out that "States Parties recognise the right of every child to a standard of living adequate for the child's physical, mental, moral and social development";
- Article 26.1 obliges States Parties to "recognize for every child the right to benefit from social security, including social insurance, and shall take the necessary measures to achieve the full realisation of this right in accordance with their national law".

Children's rights to education and health care are set down in Articles 28 and 24:

- "States will make primary education compulsory and available free to all" (Article 28.1.a)
- States Parties are to "ensure the provision of necessary medical assistance and health care to all children, with emphasis on the development of primary health care" (Article 24.2.b)

The 1989 UNCRC was followed in 1990 by the first World Summit for Children, which set seven major and 20 supporting goals for children concerning their health, education and well-being. These goals included the reduction of infant and under-5 mortality rates by a third, the eradication of polio by the year 2000, reducing deaths from measles by 95% and cases of measles by 90% by the year 1995, the elimination of neonatal tetanus and reduction of deaths from diarrhoea by 50%, a reduction of deaths from acute respiratory infection by a third, halving severe and moderate malnutrition among children under five, universal access to safe drinking water, sanitation and basic education, reduction in gender disparities, and the promotion of breastfeeding.

At the United Nations Special Session on Children in 2002, however, it was clear that progress over the decade was limited and that the international community had failed to meet most of the goals set in 1990. The main goals missed included the reduction of child mortality and under nutrition, the provision of safe water and sanitation, the tackling of child labour and the achieving of gender equity in education. Carol Bellamy, then director of UNICEF, admitted that the decade had seen "a mixture of conspicuous achievement and dispiriting failure" (UNICEF, 2002). Kofi Annan, UN Secretary General, in his report to the UN General Assembly noted "real and significant progress" was being undermined by "setbacks, slippage and in some cases, real retrogression, some of it serious enough to threaten earlier gains" (United Nations, 2001).

Despite the long history of international concern for children and their well-being and recognition of the damaging impact poverty has on children, there remains an unfortunate lack of information and statistical data on child poverty *per se* (Minujin, Delamonica, Gonzalez & Davidziuk, 2005). While there is no shortage of data on different aspects of child well-being (e.g. children in school, working children, street children and child soldiers), the lack of data on child poverty in poor countries is surprising. While a number of studies have addressed the measurement of child poverty in rich countries (Cornia, 1997; Cornia & Danziger, 1997; Bradbury & Jantti, 1999; Bradbury & Jantti, 2001; Bradbury, Jenkins & Micklewright 2001; Corak, 2005), relatively few have focused attention on how child poverty is conceptualised and measured in poor countries. Given

Child Poverty in a Developing World

data limitations and the problems associated with the collection of household income and expenditure data in poor countries, studies of poverty in developing countries often address the multi-dimensional nature of poverty by looking at health and educational outcomes, the quality of living conditions and access to basic services (White, Leavy & Masters, 2002). One study using data from the World Bank and UNICEF estimated that about 536 million children were living in absolute poverty (MacPherson, 1987), with the greatest numbers of poor children in South Asia and sub-Saharan Africa. About 70% of the absolutely poor lived in rural areas. This study had a number of limitations, however, since it used data collated from different sources (i.e. the data were not on individuals, but taken from different household surveys). The problems with measuring child poverty are manifold, not least because most indicators are based on household data and conceptualise and define poverty narrowly as low income or expenditure. Such data and methods are inappropriate for measuring child poverty, as they often do not reflect the specific needs of children adequately (Gordon, 2002; Gordon, Nandy, Pantazis, Pemberton & Townsend, 2003).

Measuring absolute poverty among children in poor countries[2]

Recognising the dearth of data on child poverty in developing countries, UNICEF commissioned the Townsend Centre for International Poverty Research at the University of Bristol to produce reliable estimates of the number of children in developing countries living in absolute poverty. To do so required a definition of

---

[2] This section will only summarise the methods and findings of what was a two-year project. Further details can be found in Gordon et al. (2003).

Poverty: Malaise of Development

absolute poverty, and the one adopted at the 1995 World Summit for Social Development [WSSD] formed the basis of the project (WSSD, 1995).

Absolute poverty was defined as:

> A condition characterised by severe deprivation of basic human needs, including food, safe drinking water, sanitation facilities, health, shelter, education and information. It depends not only on income but also on access to services. (United Nations, 1995, p. 57)

Measuring absolute poverty first required operationalising measures of severe deprivation of basic human needs, and then finding data appropriate for measuring severe deprivation. One reason for this was that conventional poverty indicators, based on household income or expenditure, are unsuited to measuring child poverty. They rely on data collected at the household level and assume that need does not vary with age and that both adults and children have identical needs and share the same standard of living (Gordon, 2002; Gordon et al., 2003).

Operationalising measures of severe deprivation

One problem with operationalising measures of severe deprivation of basic human need is the lack of international standards. While recently there have been definitions, thresholds and indicators adopted for certain basic services (e.g. the Millennium Development Goals require that people have access to "improved" sources of water and forms of sanitation, with definitions provided as to what constitutes "improved" (WHO, UNICEF & WSSCC, 2000), no such standards exist which can be used

Child Poverty in a Developing World

to reflect the "severe deprivation of basic human needs" alluded to in the WSSD definition of absolute poverty.

The concepts of poverty and deprivation are closely linked. While the former refers primarily to a lack of income and other resources that affect the quality of people's lives, the latter covers the various conditions experienced by people who are poor. Thus a child can be deprived of education, shelter, health and food, all of which will be related to (or determined by) their poverty (Gordon et al., 2003).

Deprivation can be conceptualised as a continuum, ranging from no deprivation, through mild, moderate and severe, to extreme. Different thresholds can be set for each level of deprivation, as shown in Table 1.

Table 1: Operational thresholds of deprivation for children.

Deprivation	Mild	Moderate	Severe	Extreme
Food	Bland diet of poor nutritional value	Going hungry on occasion	Malnutrition	Starvation
Safe drinking water	Not having enough water on occasion owing to lack of sufficient money	No access to water in dwelling, but communal piped water available within 200 meters of dwelling or less than 15 minutes walk away	Long walk to water source (more than 200 meters or longer than 15 minutes). Unsafe drinking water (e.g. open water)	No access to water
Sanitation facilities	Having to share facilities with another household	Sanitation facilities outside dwelling	No sanitation facilities in or near dwelling	No access to sanitation facilities

Poverty: Malaise of Development

Health	Occasional lack of access to medical care due to insufficient money	Inadequate medical care	No immunisation against diseases. Only limited non-professional medical care available when sick	No medical care
Shelter	Dwelling in poor repair. More than 1 person per room	Few facilities in the dwelling: lack of heating, structural problems. More than 3 people per room	No facilities in house, non-permanent structure, no privacy, no flooring, just one or two rooms. More than 5 persons per room	Roofless – no shelter
Education	Inadequate teaching owing to lack of resources	Unable to attend secondary but can attend primary education	Child is 7 or older and has received no primary or secondary education	Prevented from learning because of persecution and prejudice
Information	Cannot afford newspapers or books	No television but can afford a radio	No access to radio, television or books or newspapers	Prevented from gaining access to information by government, etc.
Basic Social Services	Health and education facilities available, but occasionally of low standard	Inadequate health and education facilities nearby (e.g. less than 1 hour travel)	Limited health and education facilities a days' travel away	No access to health or education facilities

Thus, food deprivation can be said to range from no deprivation, where food of sufficient quality and quantity is readily available, through to severe deprivation (reflected by severe malnutrition) and then extreme food deprivation (reflected by starvation). In the same way, measures of the different degrees of deprivation might be developed for the other basic needs mentioned in the WSSD definition.

Data to measure severe deprivation

In the past twenty years there have been a large number of high quality surveys conducted in developing countries which collect both household and individual level data. The most reliable are the demographic and health surveys [DHS] that are frequently used by organisations such as the World Bank, World Health Organisation and UNICEF (Vaessen, 1996). Other similar surveys have been run with the specific aim of collecting data on children in over 100 countries, most notably UNICEF's Multiple Indicator Cluster Surveys [MICS] (UNICEF, 1997), and the Young Lives Project (Seager & De Wet, 2003; White et al., 2002). These surveys collect information that can be used to assess the needs and well-being of children, and are increasingly being used by researchers and policy makers.

Setting thresholds
Data from the DHS and other surveys[3] were used to estimate the proportion and number of children severely deprived of basic human needs. Using the framework set

---

[3] Other surveys included UNICEF's second round of Multiple Indicator Cluster Surveys, the 1992 National Sample Survey on the Situation of Children in China, and the Russian Longitudinal Monitoring Survey.

Poverty: Malaise of Development

out in Table 1, seven measures of severe deprivation were constructed. They were:

1) *Severe Food Deprivation* – children whose heights and weights for their age were more than three standard deviations below the median of the international reference population: i.e. severe anthropometric failure.

2) *Severe Water Deprivation* - children who only had access to surface water (e.g. rivers) for drinking or who lived in households where the nearest source of water was more than 15 minutes away (e.g. indicators of severe deprivation of water quality or quantity).

3) *Severe Deprivation of Sanitation Facilities* – children who had no access to a toilet of any kind in the vicinity of their dwelling (e.g. no private or communal toilets or latrines).

4) *Severe Health Deprivation* – children who had not been immunised against any diseases or young children who had a recent illness involving diarrhoea and had not received any medical advice or treatment.

5) *Severe Shelter Deprivation* – children in dwellings with more than five people per room (severe overcrowding) or with no flooring material (e.g. a mud floor).

6) *Severe Education Deprivation* – children aged between 7 and 18 who had never been to school and were not currently attending school (e.g. no formal education of any kind).

7) *Severe Information Deprivation* – children aged between 3 and 18 with no access to radio, television, telephone or newspapers at home.

While children experiencing these deprivations are likely to be living in absolute poverty, it is possible that certain deprivations occur as a result of other factors, such as discrimination (e.g. girls not being allowed to go to school) or ill health (e.g. severe malnutrition can occur as a result of some diseases). For this reason, Gordon et al., (2003) assumed a child to be living in poverty *only* if he or she experienced two or more severe deprivations of basic human needs.

In the absence of international standards and norms concerning the needs of children, Gordon et al., (2003) followed in the tradition of Rowntree in setting thresholds so severe that few would question that they reflected unacceptable living conditions. The indicators are more severe than others used by international agencies (e.g. the threshold for severe food deprivation is set at minus three standard deviations from the international reference population, instead of the more conventional minus two standard deviations) (Nandy, Irving, Gordon, Subramanian & Davey Smith, 2005). The indicators were also designed to reflect the specific needs of children, rather than households or adults.

Results[4]

Despite setting such severe thresholds, the study found that over half of all children in developing countries (over

---

[4] The numbers and percentages presented here differ slightly to those presented in Gordon et al., (2003), because they incorporate data from surveys added later, mainly from the second round of MICS.

Poverty: Malaise of Development

one billion children) experienced one or more severe deprivations of basic human need. One in three (650 million) experienced two or more severe deprivations, and were classified as living in absolute poverty.

Figure 1 shows the proportions of children in the developing world severely deprived of basic human needs: one in three are shelter deprived (640 million), 30% are sanitation deprived (580 million), about one in five are water deprived (21%, 410 million), one in four are information deprived (22%, 347 million), one in six children under five are severely food deprived(17%, 95 million), one in seven children are health deprived (14%, 270 million) and one in eight children of school age (7-18) are education deprived (13%, 143 million).

Figure 1: Percentage of children severely deprived of basic human needs.

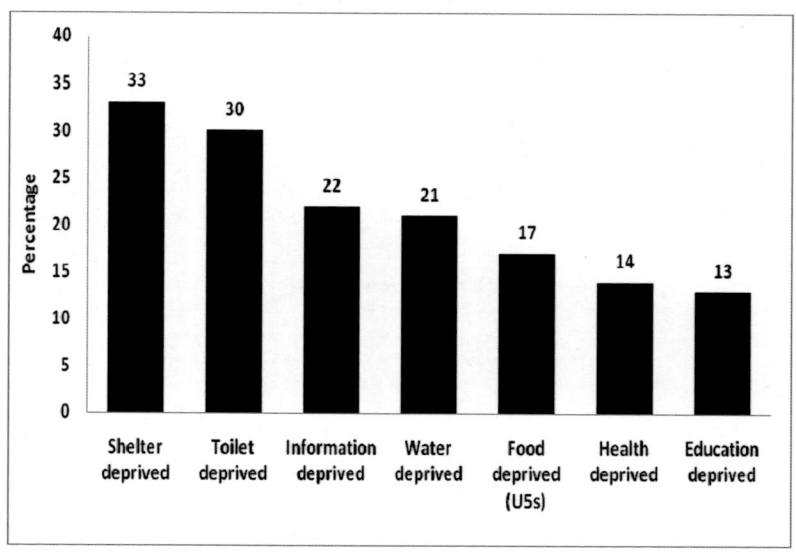

Child Poverty in a Developing World

There are considerable differences between regions (Table 2), with sub-Saharan Africa having the greatest proportion of children severely deprived of shelter (64%), water (53%), education (29%) and health (24%). South Asia had the greatest proportion of children sanitation deprived (61%), information deprived (41%) and food deprived (24%). In terms of absolute numbers, South Asia accounts for the greatest number of severely deprived and absolutely poor children.

Table 2: Regional patterns in deprivation.

Region	Category	Percentage
Sub-Saharan Africa	Shelter	64
	Water	53
	Information	40
	Sanitation	36
	Education	29
	Health	24
	Food	19
South Asia	Sanitation	61
	Shelter	45
	Information	44
	Food	24
	Health	23
	Education	19
	Water	18
Middle East & North Africa	Shelter	47
	Sanitation	45
	Information	44
	Water	24
	Education	23
	Health	19
	Food	18

Poverty: Malaise of Development

Latin America & Caribbean	Shelter	21
	Sanitation	16
	Water	14
	Information	7
	Health	7
	Food	5
	Education	3
East Asia & Pacific	Food	16
	Water	13
	Shelter	10
	Sanitation	10
	Information	7
	Health	5
	Education	4
Central & West Asia	Shelter	10
	Water	9
	Food	6
	Information	4
	Education	4
	Health	3
	Sanitation	1
Europe (Non-EU)	Food	5
	Health	4
	Shelter	2
	Education	2
	Water	1
	Information	1
	Sanitation	0

Rural areas in every region had higher rates of absolute poverty and severe deprivation, particularly for water, sanitation, education and information. This reflects the long (and continuing) neglect of rural areas in many developing countries, particularly in the provision of basic services and infrastructure (e.g. water, sanitation).

Since the data were collected at the individual level, gender differences in some deprivations can be examined. At the overall level, similar proportions of boys and girls

Child Poverty in a Developing World

experienced severe deprivation of food and health needs. The greatest differences are for education deprivation, where girls were more than one and a half times more likely than boys to be education deprived (Gordon et al., 2003, p. 22). The degree of female disadvantage was greatest in the Middle East & North Africa and South Asia regions. Studies and assessments of poverty need to examine gender differences carefully, as they often have different causes and implications; girls are more likely to be withdrawn from school in times of economic constraint, and certain behaviours (e.g. delaying medical treatment longer for girls than for boys, differences in the allocation of food, etc.) do have significant impacts on the well-being of girls and women (Evans, 1989; Behrman, 1998; Kabeer, 1994; Gürsoy, 1996). The burden of meeting family and household needs will also fall differently on children, with girls being expected to work in the home, while boys are able to go to school or work outside the home.

Child poverty in rich countries

While the study by Gordon et al., (2003) measured absolute poverty among children in developing countries, others have examined and compared the extent of child poverty in industrialised countries (Cornia & Danziger, 1997; Bradbury & Jantti, 2001; Vleminckx & Smeeding, 2001; Corak, 2005; UNICEF, 2005). Using a different measure of poverty - children in households whose equivalised annual income[5] is less than 50% of the national median - UNICEF's Innocenti Research Centre (UNICEF, 2005)

---

[5] Equivalence scales represent the consumption needs of any family type relative to the needs of a reference family, usually a single individual. Thus data are adjusted to account for family size and composition (e.g. large families with many young children, elderly couples, etc.).

Poverty: Malaise of Development

estimated rates of child poverty in 26 OECD countries (Figure 2). The lowest rates were in the Nordic countries, which have more comprehensive welfare states. The highest rates were in Mexico and the United States of America, which have less generous welfare states and less effective social safety nets.

Figure 2: UNICEF Child Poverty League of Rich Countries.

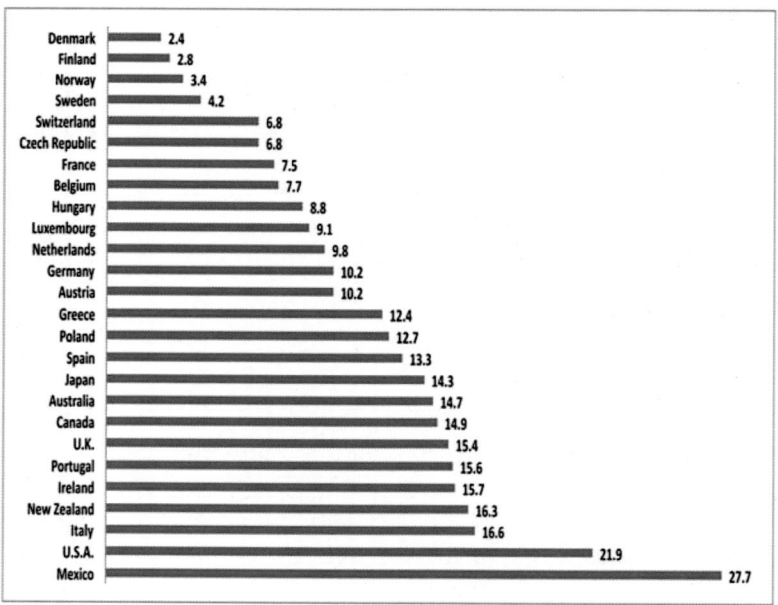

The Innocenti study also showed that child poverty increased during the 1990s in 17 out of 24 countries for which data was available (Table 3). In 16 countries, child poverty rates rose by more than 1%, and in only three countries was the decline in child poverty statistically significant (Corak, 2005). Out of those countries experiencing a decline in child poverty, only Norway had low initial rates. Child poverty, it appears, is a problem in

Child Poverty in a Developing World

both rich and poor countries, and is clearly on the rise in the former. At present, there is no way of knowing whether or not child poverty in poor countries is increasing or decreasing, since the data simply does not exist. However, recent studies suggest that during the 1990s disparities between rich and poor for a range of outcomes did increase (Minujin & Delamonica, 2003a, 2003b).

Table 3: Change in child poverty rates during the 1990s.

	Percentage point change
UK	-3.1
USA	-2.4
Norway	-1.8
Australia	-1.7
Canada	-0.4
Greece	-0.3
France	-0.2
Finland	0.5
Denmark	0.6
Sweden	1.2
Netherlands	1.7
Hungary	1.9
New Zealand	2
Japan	2.3
Ireland	2.4
Italy	2.6
Germany	2.7
Spain	2.7
Mexico	3
Portugal	3.2
Belgium	3.9
Czech Republic	4.1
Luxembourg	4.2
Poland	4.3

Poverty: Malaise of Development

Summary and discussion

This chapter has shown why child poverty merits attention as a distinct issue. Conventional measures and indicators of poverty, based on household income and expenditure data, do not address the specific needs and rights of children. Poverty is known to have extremely detrimental effects on the growth, development and well-being of children, and growing up in conditions of poverty constitutes a violation of children's basic rights. Governments and international organisations (like UNICEF and the World Bank) have an obligation to ensure that children's rights are fulfilled, and that process can only really begin by addressing the issue of poverty.

International interest in child well-being was shown to stretch back nearly a century, from the 1989 United Nations Convention on the Rights of the Child, the 1979 International Year of the Child and the 1959 United Nations Declaration on the Rights of the Child to the 1924 League of Nations' Declaration on the Rights of the Child. More recently, international interest has been signalled by doubts that the international Millennium Development Goals will be met by 2015, and by mass public campaigns like Jubilee 2000 and Make Poverty History, which focus on poverty, debt and unfair trade. In recognising the urgent need to do something about child poverty the UN General Assembly [UNGA] in late 2006 adopted for the first time an international definition of child poverty. The Third Committee of the UNGA, which deals with social, humanitarian and cultural affairs, in its report to the 61st Session of the General Assembly on the promotion and protection of children's rights (United Nations General Assembly, 2006), recognised

Child Poverty in a Developing World

> ... that children living in poverty are deprived of nutrition, water and sanitation facilities, access to basic health-care services, shelter, education, participation and protection, and that while a severe lack of goods and services hurts every human being, it is most threatening and harmful to children, leaving them unable to enjoy their rights, to reach their full potential and to participate as full members of society ... (paragraph 46).

The estimates of child poverty in developing countries presented in this chapter reflect many of the principles underlying this definition.

This chapter demonstrates how it is possible to measure absolute child poverty in poor countries, and that the greatest forms of deprivation affecting children relate to their most basic of needs: water, sanitation and housing (Figure 1). Patterns of deprivation and poverty differ between (and within) regions, with South Asia and sub-Saharan Africa having the greatest proportion and number of poor children. The different patterns of deprivation (Table 2) suggest that simple 'one-size-fits-all' policy solutions are not appropriate for dealing with the problem of poverty, and that policies need to be tailored to suit the country or region. The study found (as have others) that poverty was greatest in rural areas, although more attention needs to be paid to urban slums and shanty towns, since they are often not well represented in official statistics or survey data. This could be developed further. Why does one size not fit all? What differences emerge between poor nations in relation to potential causes?

Child poverty is not a problem restricted to poor countries, since a number of studies show quite high rates of relative poverty in rich countries (Figure 2). There is a

Poverty: Malaise of Development

worrying trend apparent in many countries, with child poverty increasing over the last decade (Table 3). Rates of child poverty were lowest in countries with comprehensive systems of social welfare and child benefit, signalling the need to increase and maintain public spending on services which impact on people (particularly children) the most: health, housing, education and employment.

UNICEF, in a number of important studies, has examined which policies work best to improve outcomes for children and reduce poverty. These studies concluded that what is needed are more equitable distributions of resources and assets (e.g. greater spending on primary education and comprehensive primary health care), better targeting of services to areas of greatest need, the collection of more appropriate and reliable data, and meeting children's basic needs (especially health, education, shelter, nutrition, water and sanitation). Also important is the need to focus on and tackle gender disparities and ensuring the rights of women and girls (Mehrotra, Vandemoortele & Delamonica, 2000; Vandemoortele, 2000; Mehrotra & Jarrett, 2002; Mehrotra, 2004). Policies need to address these issues, rather than focusing solely on economic growth and the role of markets.

Many of these policies are echoed by a recent Manifesto for International Action to Defeat Poverty (Townsend & Gordon, 2002). To tackle mass poverty, 18 courses of action are set out, the first five of which have direct implications for child poverty. These are the introduction and development of schemes to fulfil fundamental rights to social security, the legal enforcement of the right to an adequate standard of living, the introduction and strengthening of a legal right to child benefit, the adoption of a legally binding minimum level of 1% of GNP for overseas development assistance, and the establishment of a universal right of access *locally* to publicly provided basic health care and education services (Townsend & Gordon, 2002, p. 433).

Poverty is not a law of nature. It can be eradicated, through the implementation of policies and programmes that guarantee universal and equitable access to a welfare state and basic social services (as happened in Europe after the Second World War). The lives and fortunes of hundreds of millions of people in poor countries today are too important to leave to the forces of the Free Market.

References

Adekoga, N. (1994). Health care for the poor: Lessons from the USA. *African Health, 16* (5), 29-32.

Bartlett, S., Hart, R., Satterthwaite, D., De La Barra, X., & Missair, A. (1999). *Cities for children: Children's rights, poverty and urban management.* London: Earthscan/ UNICEF.

Behrman, J. R. (1998). Intra-household allocation of resources: Is there a gender bias? In United Nations, Department of Economic and Social Affairs, Population Division (Ed.), *Too young to die: Genes or gender?* (pp. 223-42). New York: Editor.

Bennett, D. L., & Eisenstein, E. (2001). Adolescent health in a globalised world: A picture of health inequalities. *Adolescent Medicine, 12* (3), 411-26.

Black, R. E., Morris, S. S., & Bryce, J. (2003, June 28). Where and why are 10 million children dying every year? *The Lancet, 361*, 2226-34.

Blendon, R. J., Schoen, C., DesRoches, C. M., Osborn, R., Scoles, K. L., & Zapert, K. (2002). Inequities in health care: A five-country survey. *Health Affairs (Project Hope), 21* (3), 182-91.

Bradbury, B., & Jantti, M. (1999). *Child poverty across industrialized nations*. Florence: UNICEF, International Child Development Centre.

Bradbury, B., & Jantti, M. (2001). Child poverty across the industrialised world: evidence from the Luxembourg Income Study. In K. Vleminckx & T. M. Smeeding, (Eds.), *Child well-being, child poverty and child policy in modern nations* (pp. 11-32). Bristol: Policy Press.

Bradbury, B., Jenkins, S. P., & Micklewright, J. (Eds.). (2001). *The dynamics of child poverty in industrialised countries*. Cambridge: Cambridge University Press.

Brewer, M., Goodman, A., Shaw, J., & Sibieta, L. (2006). *Poverty and inequality in Britain: 2006*. London: Institute for Fiscal Studies.

Carlton-Ford, S., Hamill, A., & Houston, P. (2000). War and children's mortality. *Childhood, 7* (4), 401-419.

Corak, M. (2005). *Principles and practicalities in measuring child poverty for the rich countries.* Florence: UNICEF Innocenti Research Centre.

Cornia, G. A. (1997). Child poverty and deprivation in the industrialized countries from the end of World War II to the end of the Cold War era. In G. A. Cornia & S. Danziger (Eds.), *Child poverty and deprivation in the industrialized countries, 1945-1995* (pp. 25-63). Oxford: Clarendon Press.

Cornia, G. A., & Danziger, S. (Eds.). (1997). *Child poverty and deprivation in the industrialized countries, 1945-1995.* Oxford: Clarendon Press.

Davey Smith, G. (Ed.). (2003). *Health inequalities: Lifecourse approaches.* Bristol: Policy Press.

Evans, A. (1989). *Women: Rural development gender issues in rural household economies.* Brighton: IDS Publications.

Garfield, R. (2001). Commentary: War, famine and excess child mortality in Africa. *International Journal of Epidemiology, 30* (3), 456.

Gordon, D. (2002). The international measurement of poverty and anti-poverty policies. In P. Townsend & D. Gordon (Eds.), *World poverty: New policies to defeat an old enemy* (pp. 53-80). Bristol: Policy Press.

Poverty: Malaise of Development

Gordon, D., Nandy, S., Pantazis, C., Pemberton, S. A., & Townsend, P. (2003). *Child poverty in the developing world*. Bristol, Policy Press.

Gürsoy, A. (1996). Social roles and physical health: The case of female disadvantage in poor countries. *Social Science & Medicine, 40* (2), 625-7.

Haddad, L., Ruel, M. T., & Garrett, J. L. (1999). Are urban poverty and undernutrition growing?: Some newly assembled evidence. *World Development, 27* (11), 1891-1904.

Husein, K., Khan, B. S., Omar, K., & Lobo, M. (1995). Changing patterns of child mortality in urban squatter settlements: The AKU experience. In University of the Philippines, School of Economics (Ed.), *Health sector reform in Asia* (pp. 337-338). Manila: Editor.

Kabeer, N. (1994). *Reversed realities: Gender hierarchies in development thought*. London: Verso.

League of Nations. (1924). Declaration of the Rights of the Child. Retrieved February 17, 2010 from: http://www.un-documents.net/gdrc1924.htm

Lomo, Z., & Hovil, L. (2004). *Behind the violence: The war in Northern Uganda*. Pretoria: Institute for Security Studies.

Macpherson, S. (1987). *Five hundred million children: Poverty and child welfare in the Third World.* Brighton: Wheatsheaf Books.

Marmot, M., & Feeney, A. (1997.) General explanations for social inequalities in health. *IARC Scientific Publications, 138,* 207-28.

Masmas, T. N., Jensen, H., Da Silva, D., Høj, L., Sandström, A., Aaby, P., et al. (2004). Survival among motherless children in rural and urban areas in Guinea-Bissau. *Acta Paediatrica, 93* (1), 8-9, 99-105.

Mehrotra, S. (2004). *Improving child wellbeing in developing countries: What do we know?: What can be done?* London: Childhood Poverty Research and Policy Centre.

Mehrotra, S. & Jarrett, S. W. (2002). Improving basic health service delivery in low-income countries: "Voice" to the poor. *Social Science & Medicine, 54* (11), 1685-90.

Mehrotra, S., Vandemoortele, J., & Delamonica, E. (2000). *Basic services for all?: Public spending and the social dimensions of poverty.* Florence: UNICEF, Innocenti Research Centre.

Minujin, A., & Delamonica, E. (2003a). *Equality matters for a world fit for children: Lessons from the 1990s.* New York: UNICEF, Division of Policy and Planning.

Minujin, A., & Delamonica, E. (2003b). Mind the gap!: Widening child mortality disparities. *Journal of Human Development, 4* (3), 397-418.

Minujin, A., Delamonica, E., Gonzalez, E. D., & Davidziuk, A. (2005). *Children living in poverty: A review of child poverty definitions, measurements and policies: Desk review paper for UNICEF's Conference on "Children & Poverty: Global Context, Local Solution"*, April 25-27, New York. New York: UNICEF.

Myers, R. (1992). *The twelve who survive: Strengthening programmes of early childhood development in the Third World.* London: Routledge.

Nandy, S., Irving, M., Gordon, D., Subramanian, S. V., & Davey Smith, G. (2005). Poverty, child undernutrition and morbidity: New evidence from India. *Bulletin of the World Health Organization, 83* (3), 210-16.

Reading, R., Jarvis, S., & Openshaw, S. (1993). Measurement of social inequalities in health and use of health services among children in Northumberland. *Archives of Disease in Childhood, 68* (5), 626-31.

Rice, D. P. (1991). Ethics and equity in U.S. health care: The data. *International Journal of Health Services, 21* (4), 637-51.

Roberts, H. (1997, April 12). Socioeconomic determinants of health: Children, inequalities, and health. *BMJ, 314,* 1122-5.

Satterthwaite, D., Hart, R., Levy, C., Mitlin, D., Ross, D. A., Smit, J., et al. (1996). *The environment for children: Understanding and acting on the environmental hazards that threaten children and their parents.* London: Earthscan.

Seager, J., & Wet, T. de. (2003). *Establishing large panel studies in developing countries: The importance of the "Young Lives" pilot phase.* London: Young Lives.

Siwal, B. R. (1980). Determinants and consequences of child labour. *The Nursing Journal of India, 71* (1), 15-18.

Spencer, N. (2003). Social, economic, and political determinants of child health. *Pediatrics, 112* (3), 704-6.

Strulik, H. (2004). Child mortality, child labour and economic development. *Economic Journal, 114* (497), 547-68.

Townsend, P., & Davidson, N. (Eds.). (1988). *Inequalities in health: The Black Report* (New ed.). London: Penguin. (Original ed. published 1982).

Townsend, P., & Gordon, D. (Eds.). (2002). *World poverty: New policies to defeat an old enemy.* Bristol: Policy Press.

UNICEF. (1997). *Evaluation of multiple indicator cluster surveys*. New York: Author.

UNICEF. (2000). *Poverty reduction begins with children*. New York: Author.

UNICEF. (2002). *The state of the world's children 2002: leadership: the rate of progress*. New York: Author.

UNICEF. (2005). *Child poverty in rich countries, 2005*. Florence: UNICEF, Innocenti Research Centre.

United Nations. (1989). *Convention on the rights of the child*. New York: United Nations.

United Nations, Commission on Human Rights. (1991). *Convention on the rights of the child, 1989*. New York: United Nations, Department of Public Information.

United Nations. (1959). *Declaration on the Rights of the Child*. Retrieved February 17, 2010 from: http://www.un-documents.net/a14r1386.htm

United Nations, General Assembly. (1948). *Universal Declaration of Human Rights*. Retrieved February 17, 2010 from: http://www.un.org/en/documents/udhr/

United Nations, General Assembly. (2006). *Promotion and protection of the rights of children - Report of the Third Committee*. New York: United Nations.

United Nations, Secretary-General. (2001). *We the children: End-decade review of the follow-up to the World Summit for Children*. New York: United Nations.

Vaessen, M. (1996). The potential of the demographic and health surveys (DHS) for the evaluation and monitoring of maternal and child health indicators. In M. Khlat (Ed.), *Demographic evaluation of health programmes: Proceedings of a seminar in Paris* (pp. 65-74). Paris: CICRED/UNFPA.

Vandemoortele, J. (2000). *Absorbing social shocks, protecting children and reducing poverty: The role of basic social services*. New York: UNICEF.

Vleminckx, K., & Smeeding, T. M. (Eds.). (2001) *Child well-being, child poverty and child policy in modern nations: What do we know?* Bristol: Policy Press.

Wang, L. (2003). Determinants of child mortality in LDCs: Empirical findings from demographic and health surveys. *Health Policy, 65* (3), 277-99.

White, H., Leavy, J., & Masters, A. (2002). *Comparative perspectives on child poverty: A review of poverty measures.* London: Young Lives.

Whitehead, M. (1988). *The health divide*. In P. Townsend & N. Davidson, (Eds.), *Inequalities in health: The Black Report* (New ed.) (pp. 215-381). London: Penguin.

Wood, D. (2000). Effect of child and family poverty on child health in the United States. *Pediatrics, 112* (3), 707-11.

Woolf, A. D. (2002). Health hazards for children at work. *Journal of Toxicology: Clinical Toxicology, 40* (4), 477-82.

World Health Organization. (1988). *Urbanization and its implications for child health: Potential for action*. Geneva: Author.

World Health Organization. (1995). *The world health report, 1995: Bridging the gaps*. Geneva: Author.

World Health Organization, UNICEF, & Water Supply and Sanitation Collaborative Council. (2000). *Global water supply and sanitation assessment 2000 report*. Geneva: WHO; New York: UNICEF.

World Summit for Social Development (1995, March 6-12). *The Copenhagen declaration and programme of action*. New York: United Nations, Department of Public Information.

UNAFFORDABLE RISKS AND UNAFFORDABLE PROTECTION: HOW POVERTY REDUCTION PROGRAMMES AND FOOD SECURITY STRATEGIES CAN UNDERMINE EACH OTHER

David Hall-Matthews

What could possibly be worse than poverty? Poverty limits people's productive capacity and skills; their work, ingenuity and imagination are solely focused on survival, with little prospect of a better life (Sen, 1999, pp. 87-110; Sachs, 2005, pp. 56-66). Poverty is an affront to notions of justice, freedom and modernity. As such, it provides the primary motivation for international development efforts. For those seeking to modernise developing economies, poverty is both a symbol of a failure of civilisation and a concrete brake on economic growth (Perry, Lopez & Maloney, 2006). For others, who prioritise basic needs (Ghosh, 1984), poverty is not just a malaise for development, but its antithesis. The UK Department for International Development [DFID] announced on its inception that poverty reduction would be the chief focus of its aid (DFID, 1997). Halving poverty and hunger is the foremost Millennium Development Goal [MDG].

In sub-Saharan Africa, it is now certain that the first MDG will not be met by its target date of 2015. Aid and development are failing significantly to reduce poverty. Why do poverty reduction programmes not have a greater effect? Are some people neglecting to take advantage of them, or even resisting them? Could it be that this book has its title question the wrong way round; that development is a malaise for those in poverty? Post-development writers have long argued that, for the poor, development "is a reminder of *what they are not* ... of an undesirable, undignified condition" (Esteva, 1992, p. 10); that it is

Poverty: Malaise of Development

designed to keep people in their place in the international order (Frank, 1966) and put a sticking plaster on the gaping wound of global injustice, while continuing to perpetuate it (Rahnema, 1992). This line of argument has some validity, and there are plenty of examples of pointless or harmful development programmes (Ferguson, 1994), but it is in danger of valorising poverty. Insisting on the right of the poor to be left alone – to remain poor – does not suggest much consideration of their point of view. A more useful critique of donor-funded poverty reduction agendas is precisely that: the interfering rich talk down to the poor about their unsightly, primordial poverty, without bothering to listen (Gronemeyer, 1992; Chambers, 1997, pp. 74-84; Freire, 2000). But is the experience of poverty really so subtle and complex? How can poverty reduction not be in the interests of the poor? The answer lies in this chapter's opening question. There is something worse than poverty: starvation.

This chapter considers the relationship between poverty reduction programmes and food security strategies, from the perspective of small farmers. Anti-poverty policies for the landless or urban poor, which centre on the creation of reliable employment or income generation opportunities, are outside its remit. Food security is defined by the UN Food and Agriculture Organization [FAO] as when "all people, at all times, have access to sufficient, safe and nutritious food to meet their dietary needs and food preferences for an active and healthy life" (FAO, 2009). Successful poverty reduction, sufficient to guarantee people's entitlement to food during periods of climatic, economic or political crisis (Sen, 1981) is, without question, the most effective way to maintain food security. However, for farmers who are both poor and food insecure, poverty reduction schemes may come into conflict with food security strategies. The gap between the

Unaffordable Risks and Unaffordable Protection

two agendas is clear within the structure of most international non-government organisations [NGOs], which have separate departments to deal with development and humanitarian crises. In recent years, those working in the field of famine response and prevention have increasingly sought to incorporate sustainable development agendas within their work (Buchanan-Smith & Maxwell, 1994), but this is less obvious in reverse. It remains better understood that food security requires poverty reduction than vice versa.

This is because food security is not only the absence of hunger but also, critically, the absence of the fear or risk of hunger. The food insecure will always seek to minimise risk, both by necessity and by inclination, for the simple reason that they cannot afford to lose (Hall-Matthews, 2005, p. 78-82). Any proposal that could make them richer, but might also make them poorer, will therefore be liable to be rejected. Given that the smallest annual loss has the potential to undermine their livelihoods permanently, this is perfectly sensible. They do not have the resources to speculate in order to accumulate. This does not mean to say that peasants have no interest in investing or experimenting to increase their incomes; only that, in weighing up the potential benefits of a scheme against its potential risks, they will tend to ignore the former unless they are confident about the latter. Even when the odds of success appear externally to be high, or risks low (for example if the programme involves giving farmers free seeds), smallholders may remain reluctant. The consequences of failure would be so dire that fear of it dominates their farming decisions.

This can be frustrating for governments or development agencies trying to reduce poverty. It is axiomatic that subsistence farming can only ever provide a hand-to-mouth existence. Many rural poverty reduction schemes, therefore, attempt to encourage smallholders to grow higher value crops for sale, in order to increase their incomes – and thus their food consumption. If this does not work, the underlying assumption is that peasants need to be persuaded to grow cash crops, because they are either ignorant of their benefits or prefer to stick to easier food crop farming. In other words, their inherent conservatism and irrational fear are seen as key obstacles to poverty reduction, because they run counter to entrepreneurial behaviour. Such attitudes towards poor farmers are at least as old as the concept of development itself, and were responsible, for example, for state-induced agrarian crises in colonial India, where smallholders who were unable to make a commercial profit were told that their "proper place is in the labour market" (Hall-Matthews, 2005, p. 116). Another example was the openly hostile policies that expropriated from farmers to support industrialisation in the Soviet Union (Fitzpatrick, 1994).

In the context of contemporary development, such attitudes also highlight an important difference between the aims of poverty reduction and food security. Whereas writers and policy-makers on poverty tend to emphasise the need to participate in wider markets and social networks, much recent food security literature has focused on individuals' and households' own coping strategies (Corbett, 1988; Davies, 1993). Coping strategies are not necessarily incompatible with crop diversification or community cooperation, but have a distinct objective: to avoid, minimise and manage risk. They come in different categories, at different stages, but all are based on the fear of future hunger (Corbett, 1988, pp. 1103-9; Davies, 1993, pp. 62-4). In better times, they are preventative: designed to reduce the likelihood and potential impact of food shortages – this could be by saving, finding other sources of income, or cultivating relationships with potential patrons, as well as by avoiding risk. When hardship does arise, they amount to crisis management, aimed to maintain minimum nutrition levels as safely and sustainably as possible. This might involve temporary migration on the part of some household members, or sale of inessential items, as well as reduced food consumption. Only when the threat of serious starvation emerges do people start to take final steps that might permanently affect their livelihoods (Davies, 1993, pp. 60-4; De Waal, 2005, pp. 141-71). Some impressive efforts have been made to ensure that famine relief policies support, rather than undermine, coping strategies, as well as to monitor precisely when they start to involve the taking of unwanted risks – for example, by vulnerability assessment committees in Southern Africa. This does not mean, however, that coping strategies are sufficient to maintain food security. On the contrary, they are nothing less than indicators of food insecurity, usually involving immiserisation and sacrifice.

The lengths to which poor farmers are willing to go to avoid losing their productive assets – in some cases they would literally rather starve than sell livestock, farming utensils or, above all, land – demonstrate the strength of their reluctance to lose their long-term livelihoods, which would make them much more vulnerable to future shortages (De Waal, 2005, p. 7). For food insecure small farmers, then, everything they do, at all times, is based on maintaining their grip on what they cannot afford to lose. And if you can not afford to lose, you can not afford to take risks, even if that is the only way to become richer.

Crop diversification as a poverty reduction strategy

Do poverty reduction schemes really require smallholders to take unwanted risks? If so, why? If not, why do they sometimes fail to convince farmers to adopt them? No one wants to remain poor. Contrary to some perceptions, peasants are not static or resistant to change *per se*. Poor rural households, like any others, adapt constantly to changing circumstances and respond to opportunities to increase their income. Carrying on regardless is not an option, anyway. Increasing family sizes put pressure on land, and the lack of crop rotation or fallowing degrades soil. Diverse and ingenious long-term coping strategies include off-farm work, seasonal and permanent migration by young men, cooperative use of common property resources, village support systems and making demands on local and national leaders. When they work, such strategies prevent households from sliding deeper into poverty and help them to manage occasional poor seasons, but they are unlikely to make them rich. In the many parts of Africa, in particular, where the majority of the population consists of poor farmers, there are limits to the opportunities for income diversification outside agriculture. Growing cash crops – or investing in high yielding varieties of seeds, fertiliser or irrigation to increase the output and certainty of food crops – are the most logical ways for farmers to lift themselves out of poverty. So what risks do they involve, in their eyes?

The first problem to overcome is lack of farming knowledge. While peasant understanding, in terms of which agricultural methods work best in their area, has often been shown to be just as good as that of scientists (Richards, 1985, pp. 144-9), growing unfamiliar crops inevitably presents difficulties. Most high value crops require more effort than cereals, whether in the form of extra labour or potentially expensive inputs. Even if free or subsidised seeds are given to farmers, there may therefore still be an ongoing cost to them. Well-managed programmes to promote crop diversification provide information and credit to farmers via agricultural extension services. However, it remains essential that earnings from crop sales exceed not only production costs, but also the value of food that could have been grown on the same land (the opportunity cost). This is unpredictable because, in the event of a low harvest, food prices are liable to rise steeply, whereas the value of cash crops, intended for export, will be determined by global markets, as discussed below (Hall-Matthews, 2005, pp. 57-91, 114-23). If many farmers in a given area agree to give some of their land over to non-food crops, the likelihood of local grain shortages and, therefore, high prices, becomes greater. It is just such a fear that can make subsistence farmers cautious, notwithstanding the potential benefits of higher foodgrain prices and the certainty of greater earnings from cash crops in the medium to long term.

On the other hand, it is important to remember that peasants' lack of storage facilities makes them vulnerable to food price volatility, whether they diversify or not. It is difficult and expensive to protect grains from damp and rodents, so poor farmers have to sell the majority of their crop to richer wholesalers as soon as it is harvested – when prices are at their lowest – and then buy back what they need to eat later in the year, at greater cost. This makes smallholders somewhat ambivalent about the size of their yields. In a poor local season, they will grow less but earn more per sack of grain. However, they will suffer from much higher prices – along with the landless and urban populations – when the time comes to purchase (Hall-Matthews, 1999, pp. 312-15). Real subsistence agriculture (where households eat only what they produce themselves) is, then, almost unknown. Poor farmers are in effect net grain buyers, at the mercy of overly localised trade (cheap foodgrains are usually too bulky to transport long distances on poor roads, except in emergencies), in

Poverty: Malaise of Development

which prices are as changeable as the weather, but always to their disadvantage. This is precisely why they are advised to invest in commercial crops that will give them access to wider, as well as more valuable, markets.

That raises the next critical risk of switching, partly or wholly, away from foodgrain production. How accessible and reliable are cash crop markets? In poor rural areas, all markets are imperfect, owing to a combination of poor transport and communication infrastructure and low demand. Even the grain trade often needs to be underwritten – usually highly inefficiently – by state marketing boards (which attempt to keep prices low for consumers, reinforcing the impossibility of profiting from staple farming). For traders to make the expensive effort to travel on dirt roads to remote villages to buy crops, they need to be certain that they, in turn, can sell them on, in bulk, at a profit. This may be possible for less perishable non-food crops such as cotton, tea or tobacco, as it is for cereals, but it is much more difficult for fruit or vegetables. It is a tragic irony that, in the poorest agricultural countries, agrarian markets are largely restricted to grain and non-food crops. Vegetables on sale in the major cities are often imported (and therefore expensive). This ought to present an opportunity, but markets can only be created by demand, initially from the better off, which means there needs to be an extensive middle class. A poverty reduction programme to encourage impoverished farmers in Malawi to grow capsicum on their fertile land failed on this basis. There was neither enough demand in urban areas to interest traders, nor enough production to make the peppers significantly cheaper than imported South African ones, once the cost of transporting them from remote villages while they were still fresh had been taken into account. Within a couple of years, it is probable that a market for local capsicum would have developed but farmers, who saw their supposedly valuable crops rot as they tried to sell them by the roadside, naturally returned their land to maize, after one season.

From a nutritional perspective, it would be better for farmers to grow capsicum and other vegetables for their own use, but they would still only be available for eating for a short period. Besides, smallholders reasonably calculate that, until they can grow enough staples to last the whole year, there is little logic in switching to other consumption crops, except in tiny amounts. Without the income from sales, the greater expense and difficulty of growing vegetables, which require regular watering, is hard to justify. This was illustrated by another pilot scheme in Malawi, focusing on soya. As well as advising farmers on how to grow it, and of the advantages of rotating it with maize – because it restores nitrogen to the soil – mothers were taught how to roast and grind it into a valuable nutritional supplement for their infants. However, this is a laborious process and, of 1200 people trained, only 20 actually did it. Nonetheless, households initially continued to grow soya because they were able to sell their harvest to the World Food Programme [WFP] of the United Nations [UN], which was running a child nutrition project in the area. After a few years, however, the WFP felt that it was illogical and inefficient to buy soya, mill it, and then return it to the same families. If they could be persuaded to grind it themselves, they would become self-sufficient. As soon as the WFP stopped buying it, though, most farmers stopped planting. The labour required was too much. This again emphasises that pure self-sufficiency is not smallholders' preference. What they need is reliable markets for their produce.

Governments and NGOs cannot create markets. They can, however, facilitate their development by improving infrastructure. Better communication would ensure that potential buyers from far and wide could become aware of local high prices and, conversely, that farmers would know where best to try and sell their crops. This can be done easily via local radio. Even where smallholders do not have the capacity to sell to anyone other than traders who come to them, knowledge of prevailing market prices would enable them to bargain more effectively. Equally, well-surfaced roads or railways would encourage traders to buy more from remote areas by reducing the cost of doing so. Building transport facilities is extremely expensive, however (Hall-Matthews, 2007, pp. 125-6). China is currently investing heavily in road-building in some parts of Africa and Asia, but it would be optimistic to expect these schemes to reach the poorest rural areas. Some improvements can be made locally, each year, by flattening mud roads – with the added advantage of providing temporary employment – but it is rarely enough to give smallholders access to valuable global markets, especially in large countries with low population density, such as Ethiopia or Sudan.

Even where domestic facilities do exist to enable poor farmers to sell more valuable crops in international markets, there are significant risks. Agricultural commodity prices are notoriously volatile, making it difficult to plan with any certainty. Whereas local grain markets are too small to offset the effects of variable rainfall patterns, global cash crop markets are so large that it is hard to predict levels of supply. Both have inelastic demand. Thus, a poor season for coffee or sugar in one area could coincide with a global glut, leading to low prices. In the worst case scenarios, overproduction can create long-lasting trade traps – where the market value of commodities is less than the cost of production – leaving farmers worse off than when they started (Coote, 1996). This affected coffee growers around the world, for

Unaffordable Risks and Unaffordable Protection

example, in the early years of the twenty-first century, after too many national governments had been recommended by development donors to promote diversification into coffee during the 1980s and 1990s (Gresser & Tickell, 2002). Particular problems arise when smallholders find themselves facing competition from large commercial farms with higher productivity, both within their own countries and in more developed ones. The whole strategy of poverty reduction by encouraging peasants to benefit from markets depends on their capacity to be competitive, meaning that they need to be able to make a consistent profit selling at prevailing prices. Yet, as more seek to do so, they exacerbate the existing tendency of agricultural commodity prices to fall over time.

The risks for small farmers, when presented with market opportunities to reduce their poverty, are paralleled by the experiences of national governments of poor agrarian economies. At country level, there is no alternative to international trade as a source of income, but competitiveness can be elusive. If poor nations focus on their comparative advantage in a relatively small range of transportable primary commodities, they will inevitably fall further behind industrialised nations, as demonstrated by Hans Singer and Raoul Prebisch in the 1960s (Martinussen, 1997, pp. 73-7). Influenced by this thesis, most countries have attempted to develop by investing in industry, with very varying degrees of success. Industry also creates new jobs, so many development experts argue that even countries in which the majority of the population are farmers should focus on trying to build up a reliable off-farm labour market (Bryceson & Jamal, 1997). Rural households could then send some members to work in factories, to supplement their income. If successful, the regular flow of earnings could be a useful way to ensure food security and allow farmers to take more risks. Taking

Poverty: Malaise of Development

the parallel further, however, countries can never be sure of the market for cheap industrial goods, especially now that they would have to compete with Chinese exports. Not having the capital to invest in economies of scale, product development or market research, few sub-Saharan African countries – with the partial exception of South Africa – have proved able to compete in the secondary sector, or to attract significant volumes of foreign investment to it. Even when they do, multinational companies are famously demanding of low taxes and regulations, while providing relatively few, low-skilled, insecure jobs (Kambhampati, 2004, p. 132-7). And, again, the opportunity cost should not be forgotten. Money spent directly on industrial development or on attracting investment, in the hope of enabling some people to move out of agriculture, could have been spent supporting agriculture itself.

This conundrum has become particularly pertinent in the context of recent dramatic global price rises for food and other agricultural products, following over thirty years of decline. Jacques Diouf, the Director-General of the UN Food and Agriculture Organization, has argued that this represents a long-awaited opportunity, for poor farmers and countries alike, to profit from increased global demand for cereals (Hall-Matthews, 2008a). Instead of having to seek out potentially lucrative but risky alternatives, there are now valuable markets in their areas of core expertise, if they can only access them. There are still risks, however. After decades of chronic underinvestment in agriculture, poor countries are much less competitive than those in North and South America and Central Asia, with highly mechanised farms and more productive soils and climates. This is exacerbated by the huge barriers that almost all countries have erected against agricultural trade. Until this century, the World Trade Organization [WTO]'s efforts to promote free trade were exclusively focused on industrial goods and they have yet to persuade either rich or poor nations to stop protecting their farmers with high tariffs and subsidies (Anderson & Martin, 2006, pp. 3-21). Even when developing countries have produce to sell at competitive market prices, they therefore still have difficulties in exporting it to key markets like the European Union – or even to each other.

Rich countries' subsidies to their own farmers are even more insidious constraints on free trade, because they reduce the costs of production and enable them to undercut market prices, creating poverty traps elsewhere. Massive American government support to its mere 25,000 cotton farmers, for example, has reduced the global value of cotton by 25%, making millions of more efficient producers in West Africa unprofitable. As a result, smallholder cotton production has been seriously eroded in extremely poor nations like Mali and Burkina Faso – which have nothing else to export (Gross, 2006; Hall-Matthews, 2007, pp. 121-3). The WTO was overseeing negotiations on precisely this point, with an agreement in place to abolish American and European agricultural subsidies by 2013, when the so-called Millennium Development Round of trade talks collapsed in July 2008.

Given the difficulties of competing in global commodity markets, only successful farmers in poor countries are likely to survive and profit. This may seem tautologous, but is critical to the question of whether agricultural commercialisation can effectively reduce poverty. Peasant farmers cannot all get richer in the context of price fluctuations and both domestic and international obstacles to commodity markets – and some have got poorer because of trade traps. Equally importantly, developing nations' governments have often responded to global competition by facilitating and investing in more

Poverty: Malaise of Development

efficient cash crop farming on large-scale estates. In the worst case scenarios, this has directly pushed smallholders off their land, as well as creating competition against which they cannot succeed, because they cannot match commercial farmers' investment in irrigation, seeds, pesticides or fertiliser. The best they can hope for are opportunities for seasonal labour as an alternative income source.

In the 1960s and '70s, India successfully raised national food production levels above aggregate demand and made many farmers very wealthy during the Green Revolution, which promoted high yielding seed varieties and fertiliser use – leading to calls for Africa to emulate it ever since (Djurfeldt, Holmen, Jirstrom, & Larsson, 2005). However, those farmers who could not afford expensive inputs, or who could not get official credit to purchase them on an annual basis, quickly fell behind. With others' higher yields swelling local markets, their unchanged harvests became less and less valuable, until many went out of business and became impoverished. Those who borrowed from informal money lenders to buy inputs fared little better. High interest rates and competition made many so heavily indebted that they had to hand over their entire harvest every year. Far from learning their lesson, Indian state and national governments recently encouraged poor farmers to adopt the latest expensive new agricultural technology: genetically modified seeds – again with mixed results. Thousands have found the ongoing costs to be consistently higher than the value of their yields and have committed suicide (Stone, 2002; Mohanty, 2005).

A cash crop strategy that has such polarising effects on different groups of farmers cannot be a successful way to remove poverty, even if it enhances national economies. Some poor farmers may be lucky enough to increase their earnings, but others will lose out when they cannot afford to lose. Even attempts to make food production itself more commercially successful can be counter-productive, if they fail to ensure the success of every single smallholder. If they have any say in the matter, peasants concerned about their food security are, therefore, likely to refuse to participate in the first place. Governments and development donors need to recognise, then, that there is a trade-off between agricultural investment intended to increase competitiveness and profits and that which will maintain food security. If the ultimate goal is the eradication of rural poverty, the latter has to come first. The 2008 *World Development Report*, which focused on agriculture, recognised that, while poverty had been reduced somewhat over the previous decade among farmers in middle income countries, those in the poorest countries remain poor and are further than ever from escaping their poverty traps (World Bank, 2007).

It has often been argued that trying to take advantage of trade opportunities can never be a successful development policy for the poorest agrarian economies, and still less a poverty reduction one (Dunkley, 2000; Crawford, 2001). Marxist analysis suggests that the poor have not just failed to participate in wealth generation schemes, but have been actively pushed out of them; capitalism, it is said, depends on the exploitation and exclusion of the weak by the strong (Bush, 2007, pp. 22-3). The argument of this chapter is slightly different. There will always be wealth gaps and a division between capitalists and workers, but that does not mean that poor farmers necessarily have to remain poor until capitalism has been overthrown. As argued above, even the worst off peasants could benefit from better developed markets. The problem is, in part, not that globalisation has done them harm, but that it has not reached them (Hall-Matthews, 2007). Yet this chapter has shown how commercialisation of peasant agriculture does carry inherent risks. Not only have poverty reduction programmes based on it threatened food security; rational farmers' concern to remain food secure has ensured that they have themselves undermined their chances of reducing poverty by refusing to participate. The trade-off, between wealth generation and livelihood guarantees, has not been sufficiently recognised. In many cases, food security concerns have not been taken seriously, because development agents cannot imagine anything worse than poverty – and cannot understand what they perceive to be peasants' apathetic preference to remain in it.

Combining agrarian poverty reduction and food security agendas

Are there ways to create poverty reduction programmes that also guarantee food security, making them more attractive to poor farmers? If so, why are they not used more often? Food security is not straightforward to ensure, because it can be undermined by political factors, including social unrest and conflict (Keen, 1994, pp. 11-17; De Waal, 1997, 106-32; Edkins, 2000, pp. 129-52). Individual household food security can be destroyed by very local disasters, such as fire or pests, or by the illness or death of critical family members. The HIV/AIDS pandemic has had devastating effects, increasing the risk of famines in areas previously thought to be safe (De Waal, 2007). In these circumstances, government or donor schemes that attempt to underwrite poor farmers' food security would amount to enormous social insurance policies in the context of high social risk. That would be hugely expensive – well beyond the capacity of most poor country governments, whose human and financial resource capacity has declined in recent decades (Hall-Matthews, 2007, pp. 124-6). Nonetheless, it is possible to make specific crop diversification programmes less risky for farmers by reducing their costs.

For many smallholders, as with entrepreneurs, lack of capital to invest in improved production is the primary obstacle to any attempt to augment their earnings. It is well understood that high yielding seed varieties, fertiliser, pesticide and reliable irrigation would both greatly increase average grain harvests and reduce the threat of significant crop failure in a year of low or irregular rainfall. For high value crops, such expensive inputs are indispensable. Given that a successful transition into cash crops could fairly quickly yield sufficient returns to reinvest in inputs and make a profit, large-scale schemes to encourage it are often based on cheap loans to farmers, to be repaid after a few years. Direct state investment in irrigation would be at least as expensive as in roads, but subsidised fertiliser or seeds could provide real value for money.

The problem is that they would nonetheless require large budget commitments that would be liable to overstretch government coffers in poor countries with very low revenue bases. There has been strong opposition to such schemes for many years, particularly from major aid donors such as the World Bank and DFID (Harrigan, 2008, p. 243-5). Neither domestic taxpayers, nor those in donor nations, tend to support handouts, even to the very poor. If a one-off, or short-term, input subsidy were sufficient to kick-start the smallholder economy, it could easily be justified. As has been seen above, however, it would take time before successful rural markets were developed, to enable peasants to be sure of increased income. And many economists argue that ongoing reliance on state support would discourage farmer entrepreneurialism and instead encourage a culture of dependency. There would also be a risk of favouring rich commercial farmers at the expense of

Poverty: Malaise of Development

smallholders (Howell, 2005). It would then be politically difficult to withdraw the grant system after a few years – as has been amply demonstrated by well-off farmers' resistance to abolition of the EU's inefficient and expensive Common Agricultural Policy, as well as to American, Indian and Japanese farming subsidies. If timed wrong, a sudden end to state support would again leave the weakest smallholders unable to compete.

The same problem arises, however, with government loans. It is difficult to judge when it is reasonable to expect them to be repaid, not only because some farmers will become profitable much sooner than others, but also because a credit relationship inevitably creates a conflict of interest between peasants and the state, which can potentially undermine the attempt to cooperate in poverty reduction (Hall-Matthews, 2005, pp. 114-27). Long-term loans can have a similar effect to grants on national spending plans – and can also harm smallholders if interest rates go up. The poorest countries already often have very high domestic interest rates, mainly caused, in a vicious circle, by excessive government borrowing. Short, fixed-term loans, however, put unsustainable pressure on peasants to commercialise their production within the time allowed. Even if offered at concessionary rates, this represents exactly the kind of risk they seek to avoid. A single poor harvest, caused by unfamiliarity with inputs, or a bad season, or a sluggish local market, could prevent farmers from realising enough profit to repay loans and reinvest in time, forcing them into the hands of rapacious private lenders (Hall-Matthews, 2005, pp. 116-17). Savings schemes, or microcredit, based on cooperative group lending, have been widely promoted in recent years to provide an alternative for poor households (Burra, Deshmukh-Ranadive, & Murthy, 2005), but they tend to

Unaffordable Risks and Unaffordable Protection

involve very small amounts over short periods, and have rarely been offered for farming inputs.

It is therefore unfortunate that many donor-funded agrarian poverty reduction schemes in recent decades have involved short-term loans, which effectively leave all the risk of failure with smallholders, while actually removing existing state input subsidies in order to balance national budgets. Responsible fiscal management is certainly important, but in countries with majority poor rural populations, it is illogical to sacrifice food security to it at too early a stage. Providing relief to starving rural populations in a crisis is far more expensive than any welfare scheme (Hall-Matthews, 1996, pp. 218-19; 2005, pp. 174-9; 2008b, pp. 1201-2). This demonstrates starkly how food security and poverty reduction agendas can diverge. For market-based development advisors – notably within the World Bank and International Monetary Fund – the rural poor need to be encouraged to seek out commercial opportunities by a combination of carrots (such as cheap conditional loans) and sticks (such as the removal of subsidies and guaranteed markets). The net effect of such a strategy, for some poor farmers, will be reduced income and thus fewer opportunities to buy inputs. Others will be forced to succeed in volatile, declining and poorly developed markets, of which they have limited prior knowledge. Instead of being pulled out of poverty, some will be pushed into the abyss (Hall-Matthews, 2005, pp. 78-82). Many will sensibly refuse the loans, choosing to remain poor rather than risk something worse.

There is thus a major conundrum to solve. Rural poverty reduction schemes are often rejected by their intended beneficiaries if they fail to recognise the primacy of food security; yet poverty still needs to be addressed. It would appear that programmes can only be sure to work if they are generous – particularly in underwriting the risk of

Poverty: Malaise of Development

failure – but neither national governments nor aid donors are in a position to spend heavily enough either. There are nearly 800 million food insecure people in the world – far too many to help via tax-funded welfare alone. Nor has any government ever been able to enrich its people through direct investment, though some in East and South-East Asia have succeeded by "governing the market", in support of domestic industry (Amsden, 1992; Wade, 2004). Economic take-off in the last decade in Brazil, Russia, India and China has shown that market liberalisation is necessary (Wilson & Purushothaman, 2003). Rural poverty has only been reduced slightly, however, and inequality is rising. There are still hundreds of millions of poor farmers in those countries. So can competitive markets – which, at best, offer risky opportunities for undercapitalised peasants, and often cannot be accessed at all – be harnessed to help them get out of poverty?

It is worth looking briefly at the different ways in which these governments have tried to deal with ongoing agrarian poverty. In Brazil, and especially Russia, initial success was coupled with intense economic polarisation, with narrow urban elites the main gainers (Senokosov & Skidelsky, 2001; Harris, 2005). Both have strong agricultural sectors, however, which can be expected to benefit from high food prices. Global market opportunities may, therefore, help farmers, though there remains a danger of large estates hogging the gains at the expense of smallholders. The Indian economy is particularly uneven. Economic success has been mainly driven by the high-tech and tertiary sectors, but the less competitive farming sector is much larger (Emmott, 2008, pp. 127-37). Indeed, India and China still refuse to open up their agricultural markets – one of the chief stumbling blocks in current WTO negotiations. India's increased tax base has, however, made it possible for its government to improve agrarian welfare, most notably through the National Rural Employment Guarantee Scheme, which provides up to a hundred days of work a year to supplement incomes (Sjoblom & Farrington, 2008). China is divided geographically, with most of its industrial development in the South East. Its government is seeking to encourage rural growth in its poorer Western regions through infrastructure investment and a policy of national food self-sufficiency (Fan, Zhang & Zhang, 2002). It is interesting that all four of these countries have enjoyed economic take-off from a platform of relative food security. Although agriculture has not been at the centre of their success and rural poverty is still a problem, neither poverty nor food insecurity have significantly worsened during the period of transition – though that may yet change. Of the four, food security seems most assured in China, where economic growth has been overseen by a still-communist state.

Smaller, poorer, weaker states cannot easily emulate the economic success of these huge emerging nations. However, there are some lessons to be learned. First, it remains clear that only market opportunities will help smallholders to escape poverty. But, second, they will not be able, or willing, to take those opportunities unless they are facilitated by the state. Ideally, this should involve investment in inputs, as well as transport and communication, plus welfare safety nets to guarantee food security and thus provide a platform for peasants to take risks, without fear of disaster. Far from encouraging dependency, welfare guarantees are more likely than anything to free poor farmers from negative coping strategies and stimulate their own investments in agricultural productivity and diversification. Similarly, moderate aid, in the form of free or subsidised inputs in the initial stages, is more likely to create a culture of successful farming than of welfarism. Even if some households continue to rely on employment guarantees or subsidised fertiliser for years, the supplementary income and increased yields will at least improve their food security and keep them farming. Real dependency on handouts only comes when people have lost their productive assets and become chronically food insecure (Hall-Matthews, 1996, p. 223-6). It is far better, cheaper and logistically easier – so long as institutional and political obstacles can be overcome – to provide state help early rather than late (Davies, 1996, pp. 5-9).

Most poor states cannot afford to implement all the measures required to provide a food-secure platform for development. There are, however, several policies that could reduce poverty, while anticipating risk and bolstering farmers' efforts to minimise it. First, predominantly agricultural economies should invest in agricultural production and domestic markets, as a priority over developing their industrial sector, and should ensure food sufficiency before diversifying into cash crops. High food prices will make such a strategy more popular with aid donors than it has been until now. Food security can be well supported by creating sustainable coping strategies – for example guaranteeing work between planting and harvest, paid for in cash, food or input vouchers – or by enabling households to develop their own. Simple cash transfers have proved surprisingly effective in some contexts, such as rehabilitation after floods in Mozambique in 2000 (Hanlon, 2004, pp. 378-79). Limiting the impact of bad seasons need not be expensive either. Options range from maintaining a national grain reserve to creating a weather insurance scheme, whereby farmers pay premiums in good years and receive financial support in bad (Minde, Jayne, & Ariga, 2008). Experiments in India and South Africa have attempted to create a futures market

Unaffordable Risks and Unaffordable Protection

in grain. Contrary to much misinformed comment on the 2007-08 food crisis, this kind of speculation would tend to level out prices, not increase them, and may also attract private investment in agriculture. For poverty reduction programmes based on crop diversification to work, the most useful strategy would be to provide guaranteed local markets for non-grain crops; but only if they reverse historical precedents by paying fair prices, instead of aiming to please urban consumers.

As discussed above, one of the most controversial and unsuccessful strategies to reduce rural poverty has involved the phasing out of state input subsidies. In 2005, against donor wishes, the Government of Malawi took the opposite path, distributing coupons for cheap seeds and fertiliser. Despite initial teething problems, by 2007 maize production had increased by nearly 30%, prices had fallen and there was no need to pay for imported food (Dorward et al., 2008, p. 4; Minde et al., 2008). Importantly, this was intended primarily as a food security measure, after many years of inadequate harvests and serious food crises in 2001-02 and 2004-05. It was not designed to reduce poverty by itself, though it did make many smallholders better off. The government took the view that helping farmers produce more themselves was the best way to improve their welfare, as well as reducing yield and price volatility. Although the scheme was expensive – costing $91 million in 2006-07 (Dorward et al., 2008, p. 4) – it significantly reduced the need for remedial welfare spending. The scheme presented several administrative difficulties, especially concerning the local allocation of coupons, some of which were alleged to have been sold corruptly. Whereas offering coupons in return for work building roads would have targeted the poorest farmers, the more generous distribution meant that some large estate owners also received them and gained at the expense of the state, because they would otherwise have paid for the inputs at full price (Dorward et al., 2008, p. 5). This was not disastrous, however. As all smallholders got them too, and the coupon system ensured that rich farmers were not able to buy more than their share of cheap inputs, the subsidy did not lead to Green Revolution-style polarisation. Whether Malawi now has a platform for rural poverty reduction remains to be seen, but the policy has proved very popular and has had the added advantage of stimulating extensive political debate about the issue, which can only strengthen local democracy. At a fertiliser conference in Abuja in 2007, many African and donor governments expressed an interest in replicating the Malawian programme.

Its relative success also has the potential to force international institutions like the World Bank to reconsider their long-held opposition to subsidies (Harrigan, 2008). Though some concern remains over the difficulty of either sustaining it in the long-term or ending it, there is widespread recognition that it has improved relationships between the government, private traders and smallholders, creating the potential to improve rural markets. Above all, though, a measure that was once seen as a counter-productive way to reduce poverty is now being praised for its success in increasing social protection and food security. Free market liberals can therefore acknowledge the legitimacy of state subsidy for welfare purposes, while still opposing support to American, Japanese or European farmers as an unfair barrier to trade.

Conclusion

Agrarian poverty reduction strategies commonly seek to stimulate household income by encouraging diversification into higher value crops and greater market access. For under-resourced smallholders, this process of commercialisation entails risk and increased vulnerability to climatic, economic or epidemiological shocks. This is especially the case where it is combined with the removal of input subsidies, which have been blamed for encouraging inefficient farming (Harrigan, 2008, p. 243-5). While subsistence cultivation condemns households to perpetual poverty, alternatives designed to create household growth run the risk of undercutting risk-management systems and increasing vulnerability to starvation (Dorward & Kydd, 2004; Hall-Matthews, 2005). Even if smallholders are offered cheap loans or grants for expensive seeds, the risk remains that they may not be able to find a buyer for their outputs at a price that reflects the cost of production. Moreover, if scarce land is used for cash crops that then fail to increase incomes, there will be less food to fall back on. As a result, poor farmers have often chosen not to participate in such programmes. Rational fears, that poverty reduction schemes will undermine food security, have predictably resulted in their failure.

In a controversial recent speech, Prince Charles declared that food security is more important than food production, highlighting the dangers of smallholders being crowded out by commercial estate farming ("Charles in GM 'disaster' warning", 2008). He was right, but there is no reason why food security and profitable agriculture should not go hand in hand – so long as food security is ensured first. Markets provide the only realistic opportunities for hundreds of millions of poor farmers to climb out of poverty, but governments need to facilitate and stimulate markets to minimise their risks and provide safety nets for when they fail. Rural poverty cannot be reduced by neo-liberal reliance on the market alone, but by following the social liberal philosophy of T. H. Green, John Maynard Keynes or Amartya Sen. Peasants can work their own way out of poverty if freed from the shackles of justifiable fear. The task of poverty reduction is to free them, not to mislead them with threats or incentives to take risks. The obstacle is not their lack of initiative – as too many poverty reduction strategies assume – but their simple lack of resources. They rarely have sufficient savings to invest or, more importantly, to fall back on. Poor farmers have no option but to be risk-averse, unless governments underwrite risks themselves. That is not cheap or easy, but it has been shown to be possible (Drèze & Sen, 1989). Food security ought to be a top development priority in itself. Preventing starvation is more urgent than reducing poverty. And until farmers are certain that they are food secure, poverty reduction programmes will remain ineffective anyway.

References

Amsden, A. H. (1992). *Asia's next giant: South Korea and late industrialization.* Oxford: Oxford University Press.

Anderson, K., & Martin, W. (Eds.). (2006). *Agricultural trade reform and the Doha development agenda.* Washington, DC: World Bank/Basingstoke: Palgrave Macmillan.

Bryceson, D. F., & Jamal, V. (Eds.). (1997). *Farewell to farms?: De-agrarianisation and employment in Africa.* Aldershot: Ashgate.

Buchanan-Smith, M., & Maxwell, S. (1994). Linking relief and development: An introduction and overview. *IDS Bulletin, 25* (4), 2-16.

Burra, N., Deshmukh-Ranadive, J., & Murthy, R. K. (Eds.). (2005). *Micro-credit, poverty and empowerment: Linking the triad*. New Delhi: Sage Publications.

Bush, R. (2007). *Poverty and neoliberalism: Persistence and reproduction in the global South*. London: Pluto Press.

Chambers, R. (1997). *Whose reality counts?: Putting the first last*. London: ITDG.

Charles in GM 'disaster' warning. (2008, August 13). Retrieved August 17, 2009, from: http://news.bbc.co.uk/1/hi/uk/7557644.stm

Coote, B. (1996). *The trade trap: Poverty and the global commodity markets* (2nd ed.). Oxford: Oxfam (UK and Ireland). (Original ed. published 1992).

Corbett, J. (1988). Famine and household coping strategies. *World Development, 16* (9), 1099-1112.

Crawford, G. (2001). Eliminating world poverty: Is neo-liberal globalisation the answer?: A challenge to the UK Government's White Paper. *Review of African Political Economy, 28* (88), 261-6.

Davies, S. (1993). Are coping strategies a cop out? *IDS Bulletin, 24* (4), 60-72.

Davies, S. (1996). *Adaptable livelihoods: Coping with food insecurity in the Malian Sahel*. London: Macmillan.

Department for International Development. (1997). *Eliminating world poverty: A challenge for the 21st century*. London: Stationery Office.

De Waal, A. (1997). *Famine crimes: Politics & the disaster relief industry in Africa*. London: African Rights/ International African Institute, in assoc. with James Currey, Oxford.

De Waal, A. (2005). *Famine that kills: Darfur, Sudan* (2nd ed.). New York: Oxford University Press. (Original ed. published 1989).

De Waal, A. (2007). AIDS, hunger and destitution: Theory and evidence for the 'new variant famines' hypothesis in Africa. In S. Devereux (Ed.), *The new famines: Why famines persist in an era of globalization* (pp. 90-126). London: Routledge.

Djurfeldt, G., Holmen, H., Jirstrom, M., & Larsson, R. (Eds.). (2005). *The African food crisis: Lessons from the Asian Green Revolution*. Wallingford: CABI.

Dorward, A., & Kydd, J. (2004). The Malawi 2002 food crisis: The rural development challenge. *Journal of Modern African Studies, 42* (3), 343-61.

Dorward, A., Chirwa, E., Boughton, D., Crawford, E., Jayne, T., Slater, R., et al. (2008). *Towards 'smart'*

Unaffordable Risks and Unaffordable Protection subsidies in agriculture?: Lessons from recent experience in Malawi. London: Overseas Development Institute.

Drèze, J., & Sen, A. K. (1989). *Hunger and public action*. Oxford: Clarendon Press.

Dunkley, G. (2000). *The free trade adventure: The WTO, the Uruguay Round and globalism: A critique*. London: Zed Books.

Edkins, J. (2000). *Whose hunger?: Concepts of famine, practices of aid*. Minneapolis: University of Minnesota Press.

Emmott, B. (2008). *Rivals: How the power struggle between China, India and Japan will shape our next decade*. London: Allen Lane.

Esteva, G. (1992). Development. In W. Sachs (Ed.), *The development dictionary: A guide to knowledge as power* (pp. 1-25). London: Zed Books.

Fan, S., Zhang, L., & Zhang, X. (2002). *Growth, inequality, and poverty in rural China: The role of public investments*. Washington, DC: International Food Policy Research Institute.

Ferguson, J. (1994). *The anti-politics machine: "Development", depoliticization, and bureaucratic power in Lesotho* (New ed.). Minneapolis: University of Minnesota Press. (Original ed. published 1990).

Fitzpatrick, S. (1994). *Stalin's peasants: Resistance and survival in the Russian village after collectivization.* New York: Oxford University Press.

Food and Agriculture Organization of the United Nations. (2009). *Special Programme for Food Security.* Retrieved August 17, 2009, from:

http://www.fao.org/spfs/spfs-home/en/

Frank, A. G. (1966). The development of underdevelopment. *Monthly Review, 18,* 17-31.

Freire, P. (2000). *Pedagogy of the oppressed* (M. B. Ramos, Trans.) (30th anniversary ed.). New York: Continuum. (Original work published 1968).

Ghosh, P. K. (Ed.). (1984). *Third World development: A basic needs approach.* Westport, CT: Greenwood Press.

Gresser, C., & Tickell, S. (2002). *Mugged: Poverty in your coffee cup.* Oxford: Oxfam International.

Gronemeyer, M. (1992). Helping. In W. Sachs (Ed.), *The development dictionary: A guide to knowledge as power* (pp. 53-69). London: Zed Books.

Gross, A. (2006). Can sub-Saharan African countries defend their trade and development interests effectively in the WTO?: The case of cotton. *The European Journal of Development Research, 18* (3), 368-86.

Hall-Matthews, D. N. J. (1996). Historical roots of famine relief paradigms: Ideas on dependency and free trade in India in the 1870s. *Disasters, 20* (3), 216-30.

Hall-Matthews, D. N. J. (1999). Colonial ideologies of the market and famine policy in Ahmednagar district, Bombay Presidency, c. 1870-84. *Indian Economic and Social History Review, 36* (3), 303-33.

Hall-Matthews, D. N. J. (2005). *Peasants, famine and the state in colonial Western India.* Basingstoke: Palgrave Macmillan.

Hall-Matthews, D. N. J. (2007). Does globalisation make famines more or less likely? In A. Boran & P. Cox (Eds.), *Implications of globalisation* (pp. 111-40). Chester: Chester Academic Press.

Hall-Matthews, D. N. J. (2008a). Global food price rises: Threat or opportunity for poor farmers? *E-International Relations.* Retrieved August 14, 2009, from: http://www.e-ir.info/?p=515

Hall-Matthews, D. N. J. (2008b). Inaccurate conceptions: Disputed measures of nutritional needs and famine deaths in colonial India. *Modern Asian Studies, 42* (6), 1189-1212.

Hanlon, J. (2004). Is it possible to just give money to the poor? *Development and Change, 35* (2), 375-83.

Harrigan, J. (2008). Food insecurity, poverty and the Malawian Starter Pack: Fresh start or false start? *Food Policy, 33* (3), 237-49.

Harris, J. (2005). Emerging Third World powers: China, India and Brazil. *Race & Class, 46* (3), 7-27.

Howell, J. (2005). *Farm subsidies: A problem for Africa too.* London: Overseas Development Institute.

Kambhampati, U. S. (2004). *Development and the developing world.* Cambridge: Polity Press.

Keen, D. (1994). *The benefits of famine: A political economy of famine and relief in Southwestern Sudan, 1983-1989.* Princeton, NJ: Princeton University Press.

Martinussen, J. (1997). *Society, state and market: A guide to competing theories of development.* London: Zed Books.

Minde, I., Jayne, T. S., & Ariga, J. (2008). *What role can fertilizer subsidies play in alleviating poverty and hunger? Evidence from Malawi, Zambia and Kenya.* East Lansing: Michigan State University, Department of Agricultural, Food, and Resource Economics.

Mohanty, B. B. (2005). 'We are like the living dead': Farmer suicides in Maharashtra, Western India. *The Journal of Peasant Studies, 32* (2), 243-76.

Perry, G. E., Lopez, J. H., & Maloney, W. F. (2006). *Poverty reduction and growth: Virtuous and vicious circles.* Washington, DC: World Bank.

Rahnema, M. (1992). Poverty. In W. Sachs (Ed.), *The development dictionary: A guide to knowledge as power* (pp. 158-76). London: Zed Books.

Richards, P. (1985). *Indigenous agricultural revolution: Ecology and food production in West Africa.* London: Hutchinson.

Sachs, J. D. (2005). *The end of poverty: How we can make it happen in our lifetime.* London: Penguin.

Sachs, W. (Ed.). (1992). *The development dictionary: A guide to knowledge as power.* London: Zed Books.

Sen, A. K. (1981). *Poverty and famines: An essay on entitlement and deprivation.* Oxford: Clarendon Press.

Sen, A. K. (1999). *Development as freedom.* New York: Alfred A. Knopf.

Senokosov, Y., & Skidelsky, E. (Eds.). (2001). *The Russian economy today.* Moscow: Moscow School of Political Studies, Centre for Post-Collectivist Studies.

Sjoblom, D. & Farrington, J. (2008). *The Indian National Rural Employment Guarantee Act: Will it reduce poverty and boost the economy?* London: Overseas Development Institute.

Stone, G. D. (2002). Biotechnology and suicide in India. *Anthropology News, 43* (5), 5.

Wade, R. (2004). *Governing the market: Economic theory and the role of government in East Asian industrialization* (2nd pbk ed.). Princeton, NJ: Princeton University Press. (Original ed. published 1990).

Wilson, D., & Purushothaman, R. (2003). Dreaming with BRICs: The path to 2050. Retrieved August 17, 2009, from: http://www2.goldmansachs.com/ideas/brics/book/99-dreaming.pdf

World Bank. (2007). *World development report 2008: Agriculture for development.* Washington, DC: Author.

ETHNICITY, POVERTY AND TRADE LIBERALISATION: THE KHMER PEOPLE IN SOUTHERN VIETNAM

Kirsten Besemer

Introduction

The Vietnamese population is ethnically diverse, and 13-14% of the people in Vietnam are considered to belong to one of about 54 ethnic minority groups (Van, Son, & Hung, 2000; Tinh, 2001). The Khmer people are one of these many ethnicities. Ethnically and culturally related to the Cambodian people, the Khmer differ from the majority Vietnamese population, the Kinh, by their physical features, language, culture and religion. Since Vietnam's reunification, these differences have been the source of simmering ethnic tension. While Vietnam has been experiencing rapid economic growth since the 1980s, the poverty rate of the Khmer remains stubbornly high, resulting in a widening poverty gap between the Khmer and majority Kinh ethnic groups (AusAID, 2004).

In recent years, trade liberalisation has given a new form to the Khmer people's economic exclusion. Well integrated in international markets, the Mekong Delta area has been strongly influenced by international competition. For farmers, however, the ability to be integrated in international markets depends on access to production factors such as enough land, capital, and other resources needed to produce at a sufficiently high level. Additionally, farmers need social capital and access to sufficient information to participate in export production (Taylor, 2007). Using a livelihood-centred approach, this paper uncovers some of the mechanisms through which trade liberalisation has exacerbated existing ethnic

Poverty: Malaise of Development

inequality in the Mekong Delta by increasing the importance of those assets of which ethnic minorities possess least. The chapter uses fieldwork results obtained from focus group interview discussions among Khmer communities in two Vietnamese provinces, An Giang and Soc Trang. The study included 14 focus group discussions, five of which were conducted in An Giang and the other nine in Soc Trang province[1]. This fieldwork is complemented by interviews with ethnic Kinh farmers in An Giang province.

The results of this research show that marginalisation of the Khmer people is a consequence of a number of factors that place them at a disadvantage. This marginalisation is likely to increase as a result of trade liberalisation, because Khmer people lack the factor endowments they need to cope with the changing economic climate. This chapter will look at the tangible and intangible assets of Khmer ethnic minorities in the Mekong delta, and the extent to which these assets influence the way people are affected by trade liberalisation policies. The chapter will also discuss some of the future implications of a widening ethnic poverty divide. Some of these implications are already becoming apparent. In recent years, increasing poverty and landlessness among Khmer Krom ethnic minorities have given rise to land rights protests and disputes over land (Taylor, 2004b). Unless circumstances change, increasing ethnic divisions are likely to lead to increasing political

---

[1] I was not involved in any aspect of the planning or execution of the qualitative fieldwork, but have analysed the raw fieldwork data obtained with the permission of the researcher who carried out the fieldwork, Signe Madsen. This chapter could not have been written without her generous help. The surveys and interviews with ethnic Kinh farmers and interviews with local authorities referred to in this chapter are my own work.

Ethnicity, Poverty and Trade Liberalisation

instability, social unrest and greater economic inequality. This chapter will argue that, while the inequality of the ethnic Khmer people is not caused by trade liberalisation, trade liberalisation intensifies existing inequalities based on ethnicity, gender and religion. Political institutions need to look beyond cultural simplifications in order to address the underlying causes of ethnic inequality and protect those who are most vulnerable to marginalisation during economic reform.

The distributional effects of trade liberalisation in Vietnam

Trade liberalisation has been one of the latest steps in Vietnam's economic transition from a centrally planned economy to a capitalist market system. This process began in the early 1980s when, facing a severe economic crisis, the government began to decollectivise agriculture and move towards household-based production. Through a series of reforms referred to as "Doi Moi" or "renewal", restrictions on internal trade were gradually removed, until households were able to own, sell and rent out land, and choose the way they used their land and where they sold their harvests. The late 1980s and early 1990s were characterised by major cuts in government spending and a removal of most of the restrictions on foreign direct investment. By the mid-1990s, foreign investment had become about one third of all investment in Vietnam. At the same time, reductions in government spending resulted in the removal of subsidies from a range of local industries (Beresford, 2003). The government subsequently proceeded to liberalise external trade through tariff reductions and the removal of the need for permissions to trade (Nguyen Ngoc, 2006). Throughout the 1990s and into the new millennium, more restrictions on imported and exported goods were removed, as Vietnam entered into a

Poverty: Malaise of Development

number of bilateral and multilateral trade agreements. The most important of these included membership of the Association of South East Asian Nations [ASEAN] in 1995, membership of the Asia-Pacific Economic Cooperation [APEC] in 1995, the bilateral trading agreement with the USA in 2000 and membership of the World Trade Organization [WTO] in 2007 (Nguyen, T. D. & Ezaki, 2005). In aggregate economic terms, Vietnam can be seen as a success story of economic transition. Since the beginning of Vietnam's Doi Moi period, there has been an extraordinary growth in the gross domestic product, which at times peaked at over 8%. At the same time, there has been a sharp reduction in the number of low-income households, particularly during the reforms of the 1990s. More than a quarter of households in Vietnam that were poor in 1992-93 moved above the official poverty line in 1997-98 (Justino & Litchfield, 2002; Kabeer & Van Anh, 2006). Such aggregate figures conceal the fact that gains from these developments have been far from equal. Trade liberalisation has resulted in a rapidly increasing disparity between rural and urban areas, with cities capturing most of the benefits. Throughout the 1990s, as restrictions on imports and exports were removed, inequality between provinces rose. In other words, Vietnam's trade liberalisation process has been accompanied, not only by rapid economic growth, but also by rising inequality.

The impact of this rising poverty divide can be regarded in different ways. On the one hand, compared to most countries, Vietnam remains relatively equalitarian (T. Nguyen, T., Le, Vu, & Nguyen, T. P., 2006). On the other, the rate of increase in inequality is quite high, and some researchers warn that, unless the government responds with redistributional fiscal measures, levels of inequality in Vietnam could become the highest in Southeast Asia within the next ten years (Fritzen, 2002; Jensen & Tarp,

2005). Moreover, it is also highly significant that the ethnic Kinh have been far more likely to escape poverty than people from minority groups. As a consequence, the difference in poverty rate between the majority population and ethnic minorities has increased considerably (World Bank, 2003; Nguyen, T., et al. 2006; Heo & Doanh, 2009). The social significance of the ethnic poverty divide becomes even clearer when expressed in absolute terms. Though only one in eight Vietnamese belong to an ethnic minority group (Van et al. 2000; Tinh, 2001), there are 6.2 million poor people from ethnic minorities and 9.5 million poor people from the Kinh ethnic majority group (Nguyen, T., et al. 2006). When poverty is calculated through food intake, the disparity is equally great, as approximately 43% of the chronically food poor are from ethnic minority groups (Baulch & Masset, 2003). In conclusion, poverty in Vietnam is increasingly becoming an ethnic minority issue.

While opinions about the relationship between inequality and trade liberalisation are divided, there appears to be a theoretical logic to the view that there is a positive relationship. Removing restrictions and incentives to imports and exports will restructure the economy. Therefore, by its very nature, trade liberalisation requires adjustment. The requirements of adjustment generate distributional effects, as those households and individuals who are in a good position to make adjustments will receive more of the gains from trade liberalisation, while those unable to adjust to changes are more likely to suffer adverse effects (Winters, McCulloch, & McKay, 2004). An analysis of poverty in Vietnam during trade liberalisation therefore needs to centre on the differences in people's capability to adjust to the changes it brings.

Poverty: Malaise of Development

Trade liberalisation and adjustment

For the purposes of this chapter, the focus will be on the way *rural* households adjust to external shock, as nearly all Khmer minority people live in rural areas. The types of shocks generated by trade liberalisation can be differentiated in a number of separate effects. Firstly, trade liberalisation is likely to have an effect on prices. Typically, a lifting of restrictions will decrease the prices of imports and increase the prices of exports. The extent to which households really experience these effects will depend on the way prices are transformed before they reach the household level. The quality of infrastructure, geographical factors, the number of "middlemen" and the way the domestic market behaves can result in large differences in prices between different parts of the country (Hertel, 2006). For farming households, price shocks will change the income generated by the crops produced and the cost of farming inputs and household consumption. Changes in this relationship can either increase or alleviate financial poverty. Households may therefore need to adjust to price changes by changing the type or amount of crops produced or by changing consumption patterns. The levels of education of adults in the household and their access to relevant information are likely to determine the household's ability to make such changes successfully.

A second effect of trade liberalisation is that it often leads to the creation of new markets and the disappearance of former markets (Winters et al. 2004). A household's ability to respond to such changes will typically depend on its ability to switch production or to make production more efficient in a market that has become more competitive. Changing crop types requires knowledge, both the knowledge of which crops are profitable and the knowledge of how to produce new crop types. Changing crops may also create changes in the need for labour, and may therefore depend on a household's ability to provide this labour. Improving efficiency may require a combination of knowledge and resources. Also, such changes will typically require some investment, which may be substantial; for instance, when switching from agriculture to aquaculture. In some areas, land may only be suitable for a small variety of crops, so geographical location will also affect the ability to change production, as will the knowledge and networks to facilitate the effective sale of products.

The above are the most immediate effects of trade liberalisation. However, trade reform is normally accompanied by a range of changes that are directly and indirectly related. For example, as part of trade liberalisation, Vietnam has also removed trade-related restrictions on foreign investment (Binh & Haughton, 2002). Vietnam's increasing integration in the regional and global economy has also contributed to the amount of foreign direct investment, because it raised investors' expectation that investments in Vietnam would be profitable (Nguyen, T. D., & Ezaki, 2005). As in most developing countries, few rural households in Vietnam use farming as their sole source of income. The majority of farmers augment income from farming with various forms of rural, non-farm employment. There are likely to be more of such opportunities as a result of Foreign Direct Investment [FDI] flows following trade liberalisation, as FDI is typically concentrated in manufacturing industries, creating a greater demand for rural off-farm labour (Reardon, Stamoulis, & Pingali, 2007). On the other hand, farmers who are, for various reasons, unable to take advantage of off-farm rural employment opportunities are more likely to be left behind as a result. Typical reasons for an inability to gain access to rural non-farm

Poverty: Malaise of Development

employment might be a lack of education, distance from off-farm employment opportunities, or the lack of knowledge and social networks to know and avail oneself of rural non-farm employment opportunities.

Policies to attract more foreign investment and policies to promote exports have also spurred investments into Vietnam's road system. In many parts of Vietnam, and particularly in the Mekong Delta, there are large areas unconnected by a road system and, where roads do exist, they are of poor quality. The building of roads is normally regarded as a good policy, as low quality and inadequate roads lead to higher transaction costs in the rural economy (Reardon et al. 2007). Such availability does not necessarily bring benefits to people living near the area where roads are planned, however, as fieldwork results will demonstrate later in this chapter.

The previous section shows that many of the assets required for successful adjustment to trade liberalisation correspond to the characteristics that divide rich and poor in many developing countries. In their ground-breaking paper, Chambers and Conway (1992) defined the main components that determine the gains or outputs from a livelihood. These are:

- People's repertoire of capabilities; the knowledge they need to earn a living;
- Intangible assets, such as claims and access to services, access to information and access to knowledge; for instance about new seeds or new technologies;
- Tangible assets, such as land, cash savings and machinery (Chambers & Conway, 1992).

The same three aspects are essential in order to adjust to changes caused by trade liberalisation policies. As shown in the preceding section, invisible assets, such as knowledge, education and social networks, are as essential as tangible assets, such as sufficient, conveniently located, high quality land and the resources to invest in it. Trade liberalisation, by causing changes, favours those who are most flexible. Being flexible requires certain resources, but also the knowledge of how to use them and access to sources of information and support.

Conversations with many Kinh rice farmers in various locations in the Mekong Delta consistently showed that these characteristics are not widespread. The majority of farmers found that insufficiently large areas of cultivable land, lack of training, lack of resources to mechanise and insufficient resources to afford increasingly expensive inputs pushed down the profit margin of farming to a minimum. Many expressed serious concern about their ability to continue making a living in these circumstances, and were looking for alternative livelihoods, either for themselves or for their children. They often sought to augment their minimal income from farming through on-farm and off-farm diversification. All of these problems are further complicated for Khmer people, as their ability to derive a sustainable livelihood from their land is restricted by much lower levels of education, a poor ability or even inability to speak Vietnamese, and a lack of access to markets, information and knowledge. These same factors also limit Khmer people's ability to diversify and find additional sources of income.

A 2001 study by Van de Walle and Gunewardena found that, though there are major differences in tangible productive assets between ethnic minority and majority households, this difference alone cannot explain the difference in poverty between the two ethnic groups. Even compared to households with "comparable household characteristics", minority households tend to be worse off.

Poverty: Malaise of Development

In places where they live in similarly inhospitable and geographically remote areas, with similar amounts of land as the people of Kinh ethnicity, the minorities are still more likely to be poor than those living in similar circumstances (Van de Walle & Gunewardena, 2001). In fact, according to an analysis by World Bank researchers, differences in tangible assets can only explain one third of the poverty gap between ethnic minorities and Kinh people (Baulch, Chuyen, Haughton, & Haughton, 2002). In other words, minority households have lower returns on their productive assets. This suggests that intangible assets are very important in understanding the mechanisms behind the ethnic differential. For the purposes of this chapter, intangible assets are first disaggregated into political and social factors. A subsequent section will look at the relationship between intangible assets, tangible assets and economic outcomes during trade liberalisation.

Political tensions and their repercussions

An understanding of the Khmer's particular political situation first requires an understanding of the political position of ethnic minorities in general. At best, it can be said that the Vietnamese government has an ambiguous attitude towards the ethnic minorities living within its borders. On the one hand, Vietnam has long recognised the citizenship of the ethnic minority people living on Vietnamese territory, and discrimination against ethnic minorities is prohibited in the constitution (McElwee, 2004). In spite of this, the existence of ethnic minorities in Vietnam remains a highly sensitive political issue. This sensitivity is illustrated by the absence of ethnic minority studies as an area of academic enquiry in Vietnam. In fact, there is no recent accurate census of the characteristics of ethnic minorities currently living in the country. The last national survey of Vietnamese minorities, recorded by the General Department of Statistics in 1979, found 54 ethnic groups, speaking a variety of languages belonging to five different Southeast Asian language families. Although the list of ethnic groups recorded in 1979 is now widely acknowledged to be inaccurate, outdated and oversimplified, there has been no large-scale census of ethnic groups since then (Ba, Hanh, & Cuong 2002; McElwee, 2004). Apart from censuses, there is a general lack of research about the characteristics of the different minority groups. Some of this apparent lack of interest might be related to the barriers researchers face when attempting to do research on ethnic minority populations. Both Vietnamese and foreign researchers typically have great difficulty persuading the authorities to allow research on ethnic minority people (Scott & Lloyd, 2006; Human Rights Watch, 2009), and during my own fieldwork I, too, was frequently advised to avoid studying ethnic minorities, as research permission would be much more likely to be withheld.

There are some historical roots to the sensitivity of ethnic minority issues. During the French colonial period, Vietnam was often portrayed as a highly primitive culture. French texts portrayed Vietnamese society as fragmented and divided, using this as an argument to explain the ease with which it was conquered by various foreign invaders. As a colonial power, the French researched ethnic differences in great detail, stressing the great diversity of cultures and ethnicity in Indochina and dismissing the notion of Vietnam as a single entity. To distance themselves from colonial writing, and in an effort to erase the unflattering image such writings presented of Vietnam, revolutionary writers responded with strong assertions of Vietnam's unity and uniqueness (Pelley, 1998). In this context, for researchers to focus on ethnic minorities as an

Poverty: Malaise of Development

area of study still challenges the idea of Vietnam as a single culture and country. As a consequence, ethnic minorities do not get much attention in either research or policy discourse (Tinh, 2001). For Vietnamese researchers, the relationship between ethnicity and poverty may in itself be a reason to avoid the subject, as ethnic minorities have increasingly come to represent a flaw in Vietnamese policy-making. By their omission from mainstream academic and policy discourse, ethnic minority people's difference is further enhanced. For policies to target adequately the specific problems that ethnic minorities face, good knowledge is a first prerequisite. The current literature on ethnic minorities in Vietnam is scarce, and there is a lack of evidence about the factors that cause the disadvantages faced by Vietnam's ethnic minorities.

With regard specifically to the Khmer Krom ethnic minority people, it is not only a lack of research that has led to considerable factual inaccuracy. Much of what is known about the Khmer Krom is disputed, because the facts surrounding the Khmer people's presence in Vietnam have considerable political significance. For example, according to official Vietnamese statistics, there are a little more than one million Khmer people in Vietnam, the vast majority of whom live in the Mekong Delta. Khmer Krom leaders put the number at about ten million, and claim that another 1.5 million Vietnamese Khmer have now fled to Cambodia (UNPO 2009a).

One of the most important controversies regarding the Khmer Krom relates to their history, particularly to the question of whether the Khmer Krom are the original inhabitants of the Mekong Delta, or whether they are immigrants to Vietnam. This problem is highly complicated, as there is very little historical evidence from the time in which the Mekong Delta region first became inhabited (Peang-Meth, 1991). What is clear, however, is that the lower reaches of the Mekong Delta were once part of the Khmer Empire, which dominated South-East Asia for six hundred years before it fell into decline in the 15th century (Coe & Cof, 1957).

The word "Khmer Krom" means lowland Khmer. The reference to the Khmer as southerners relates to the concept of the Khmer Krom as part of a vision of Cambodian lands that follows the territory of the former Khmer Empire. The old imperial borders stretched from North to South along the Mekong River, including the Cambodian hill tribes, referred to as the "upland Khmer"; the "Khmer Islam", Muslims living in the middle reaches of the Mekong River; and the Khmer Krom, most of whom live in what is now called Vietnam (Ovesen & Trankell, 2004). In Cambodia, the Khmer-inhabited part of the Mekong Delta is known as Kampuchea Krom, a Cambodian territory which they allege to have been unlawfully occupied by Vietnam since the 17th century, after the fall of the Khmer Empire. Collective indignation about Vietnam's occupation of Kampuchea Krom is an important part of Cambodian national identity, and the dispute over the lower Mekong Delta area is the main reason for the continued enmity between Cambodia and Vietnam (Clayton, 2006). Presumably, it is for this reason that Vietnamese people tend to refer to the Khmer minorities simply as "Khmer" rather than as "Khmer Krom".

Khmer Krom people in the Mekong River Delta have frequently in the past formed nationalist movements, which aimed to reunite Kampuchea Krom with Cambodia, to recreate the old borders of the former Khmer Empire. The Vietnamese government is conscious of the possibility that a new Khmer nationalist movement may form at any time and therefore reacts strongly and aggressively to any expressions of discontent or nationalism among the Khmer

Poverty: Malaise of Development

ethnic minorities (Human Rights Watch, 2009). Various rights groups and Khmer activists accuse both the Vietnamese and Cambodian governments of using violence to suppress the freedom of Khmer people to practise their religion and retain their language, culture and identity (UNPO 2009b). Khmer groups frequently complain about alleged human rights abuses by the Vietnamese government against their people, including the torture and unlawful killing of prisoners of conscience. The Vietnamese government officially rejects all allegations of suppression, discrimination or restrictions of rights of ethnic minority peoples. In various Vietnamese publications, such as the Communist Party newspaper, government representatives allege that foreign organisations, such as the Geneva-based Vietnam Human Rights Committee, Human Rights Watch and the United Nations, deliberately publish fabricated information about supposed Vietnamese human rights abuses ("Vietnam rejects false report ...", 2009; "Vietnam rejects Human Rights Watch's fabrication", 2009). However, regardless of which side one chooses to believe, the steady stream of Vietnamese Khmer refugees seeking asylum in Cambodia and Thailand suggests that there are some problems.

To sum up, the political situation of the Khmer people is dominated by the perception that they form several distinct threats to Vietnam's stability. First of all, they are a potential source of social unrest and a national security risk. Secondly, they are a potential source of criticism against Vietnam's economic policy. Thirdly, the perception of ethnic minorities as being separate from the Kinh/Hoa people threatens to undermine the idea of Vietnam's unity. Perceived as 'Vietnam's enemy from within', the political uneasiness surrounding the Khmer people impedes their assimilation into Vietnamese society. Moreover, the fear of any discontent being expressions of nationalist tendencies has led to a repression of legitimate development concerns voiced by Khmer people, depriving them of a way to communicate their development needs and to contribute to solutions to their economic deprivation.

The tacit hostility between the ethnic Kinh and Hoa and the Khmer minority people has also influenced public discourse. Khmer people are often described in culturally fundamentalist ways, using primordialist notions to explain the Khmer people's economic marginalisation. In *Farmers, agriculture and rural development in the Mekong Delta of Vietnam*, which only mentions the Khmer people once in its 200 pages, the vulnerability of the Khmer people is explained as being the result of the following causes: "... less access to information, low education, strong belief and tradition, less sensitivity to changes and a large percentage of them are poor." (Nguyen Ngoc, 2006). In a later chapter, Nguyen Ngoc emphasizes the characteristics of the majority ethnic group in the Delta, the Kinh people: "The personal characteristics of the *Kinh* people in the Mekong Delta are known as *communal responsibility, self-control and confidence, creative dynamism, adventure, liberation and generosity, bravery and straightness, and value of equity* [Emphasis in the original]" (2006, p. 193). The fact that such a blatantly racist statement could be published in Vietnam suggests that such attitudes may not be unusual or, in any case, can go unchallenged. The statement also lends credence to allegations by the Khmer people that they are discriminated against in Vietnam. In May 2009, thousands of Vietnamese Khmer Krom people staged a demonstration in Geneva, alleging that they were the target of organised discrimination and expropriation by the Vietnamese government.

In a similarly culturally fundamentalist notion of the causes of poverty, Vietnamese writing frequently relates ethnic minority poverty to religion. While most

Vietnamese are Mahayana Buddhists, the Khmer are usually Theravada Buddhists. This difference in religion is sometimes seen as part of the reason for poverty among the ethnic Khmer people. For instance, in a Vietnamese report written for UNESCO, poor health is related to "superstition", rather than lack of access to the medical system. "When children get sick, they [the minority people] are only treated at home by traditional methods, that include prayers to the ancestors, which are certainly ineffective, that mainly rely in a superstitious belief" (Nguyen, V. P., 2009). In reality, focus group discussions revealed that the Khmer people did not always know where to go to access medical health services, owing to problems of language and access to information.

Some foreign publications have taken over the idea that Khmer culture itself is a cause of poverty. An AusAID publication states that one cause of the greater incidence of poverty among the Khmer people is that: "Khmer social institutions (of culture, religion, and customs) may have a great impact on livelihoods and poverty reduction capacity within the Khmer community" (UNDP & AusAID, 2004), though it does not go on to explain through what mechanisms culture, religion or customs contribute to poverty. There has been no academic study demonstrating direct linkages between culture, customs or religion and the economic deprivation of ethnic minority people as such, though it might be argued that the ongoing conflicts between Khmer and Kinh people about the right to practise customs and religious observances could potentially contribute to economic deprivation. More importantly, however, culturally fundamentalist notions of ethnic minority poverty undermine the effective targeting of policy to narrow the ethnic poverty divide, as essentialist notions of poverty leave little room for the agency of such "superstitious" or "culturally backward" people.

The repression of Khmer protests, the Khmer people's perception that the Vietnamese are settler colonists on Cambodian lands, and the Khmer people's perception that they are discriminated against by the majority population, have been strong deterrents against their successful integration into Vietnamese society. In response to the negative perceptions of the Vietnamese majority population, Khmer communities have emphasised their isolation and ethnic difference (Taylor, 2004a). One of the most obvious channels through which this isolationism affects Khmer people's livelihoods is language. The next section will discuss the way access to education and information, and command of the Vietnamese language, affects people's level of access to educational, political and economic resources.

The social mechanisms of ethnic inequality

Poor command of Vietnamese affects vulnerability in a number of different ways, and was a recurrent topic in all focus group discussions. Conversations with Khmer people in different localities revealed that language had a major effect on people's ability to benefit from the channels of information available to them and to participate in local decision-making processes. For instance, Khmer people are often marginalised from the possibility of participating in mainstream grass-roots organisations, including the Women's Union, as well as any local decision-making processes, such as village meetings. At the heart of this problem lies not only an inability to express oneself, but also shame at exposing one's lack of education. Focus group participants felt that knowledge was essential to be

Poverty: Malaise of Development

able to participate in meetings, and therefore would keep quiet if they felt their knowledge to be insufficient.

Village meetings are the result of Decree 29, a government initiative which introduced grass-roots democracy at the local level in 1998. Such meetings provide one of the few possibilities villagers have of participating in the community decision-making process, and village meetings are sometimes used as participatory tools for development planning. Also, village meetings are the main way in which the government communicates its own plans and policies. The village meetings provide a forum for villagers to find out about local issues that concern them, including whether or not infrastructure projects are planned for their area (Mattner, 2004; UNDP & AusAid, 2004). Apart from communicating government plans, village meetings are also used, both by the government and by NGOs, to inform people about a range of topics, including irrigation methods, crop types, the importance of drinking safe water, how to avoid mosquito-borne illnesses and where to go for medical assistance.

In particular, Khmer women reported a lack of confidence in speaking out in meetings as their greatest deterrent. Even women who were able to speak Vietnamese were far more insecure about their ability than men whose language skills were at a similar level. Typically, Khmer people have more segregated gender roles than ethnic majority people, probably owing to their isolation as much as to any particular cultural differences. Women generally receive even fewer years of education than men and levels of illiteracy are very high.

According to focus group participants, the availability of translators in public meetings varied according to local custom. In some places, translators would be made available, in others local villagers who spoke both Khmer and Vietnamese would volunteer to translate, while in other places translators were not made available at all. In the focus group meetings, it became clear that participants would not normally ask for a translator if their knowledge of Vietnamese was limited, as participants were embarrassed to reveal their "ignorance" or lack of education. As one Khmer woman from An Giang province said, about village meetings: "I just listen in the meeting, because I cannot express myself clearly in Vietnamese." If, like many Khmer people, her understanding of Vietnamese was limited as well, she might not have understood all of what was discussed at the meetings either.

The focus group discussions clearly demonstrate the importance of education as a way of preventing vulnerability. Shame, lack of confidence and lack of knowledge were mentioned as a direct consequence of having little or no education, and all of those reasons were listed as reasons for not participating in village meetings. In itself, this result is unsurprising. Khmer school enrolment rates are much lower than those of the Kinh people. In primary schools, 77.3% of ethnic Khmer boys and 75.3% of ethnic Khmer girls are enrolled; in lower secondary schools, this percentage plummets to only 23.8% and 21.2% for boys and girls respectively. These figures are dramatically lower than those for ethnic Kinh people, with 64.8% of Vietnamese students enrolled in lower secondary education (Baulch, Chuyen, Haughton, & Haughton, 2007).

The lack of education of Khmer minority students is not the result of poor availability of schools. Khmer students typically have much higher drop-out rates than ethnic Vietnamese students living in the same area. In an article in the international Vietnamese paper *Vietnamnet Bridge*, a reporter suggested that Khmer pupils were "dropping like flies" out of school, because of an "inability to learn", "fear of school" and the need to help their parents earn a living ("SOS: Pupils dropping like flies ...",

2008). The article is interesting both for its conclusions and for the condescending tone in which it is written. Focus group discussions revealed that parents, especially mothers, were deeply concerned about their children's progress in school. Some women expressed the hope that their children might find jobs outside farming, for instance as hairdressers, but were also pessimistic about their children's chances. Owing to the strong gender divisions that operated in the community, it was considered a woman's job to help children with their homework. Because women had fewer years of education than men, they felt helpless to assist their children with their learning. Normally, the children do not speak Vietnamese when they start school, so being taught in Vietnamese places them at a considerable disadvantage. There are very few teachers from ethnic minority backgrounds and Vietnamese teachers very rarely speak Khmer. It is then understandable that, being placed in a foreign-language teaching environment without the ability to understand lessons, school might be a frustrating, or even intimidating experience for the Khmer minority pupils. While it may seem that difficulties in doing well at school and being needed to work at home are different reasons for schoolchildren to drop out, the two factors are highly related. If a child does not enjoy school, is not making good progress and is therefore not expected to get good results, the opportunity cost of removing them from school to help with farm work is much lower. Similarly, if pupils and teachers believe that a child is likely to drop out early, there are fewer incentives for either to work towards good results. Moreover, negative perceptions of Khmer people, like the comparison with "flies" in the article, are likely to create a negative atmosphere for Khmer pupils in Vietnamese schools.

Ethnicity, Poverty and Trade Liberalisation

While language is one barrier to Khmer people's ability to participate, strong gender divisions also have a major effect on Khmer communities' ability to lift themselves out of poverty. Focus group discussions showed that Khmer men and women tended to segregate topics according to men's and women's issues, and ascribed strong importance to the male role of head of the household and representative of the family. Both men and women believed that going to village meetings was the responsibility of the head of the household. Interestingly, while people believed this was how it ought to be, in reality women did attend many of these meetings in their husband's place. In one of the focus groups, the head of the hamlet observed that the number of women at village meetings was in fact greater than the number of men who attended. His explanation for this was that women had more time than men and were therefore in a better position to leave the house. When constructing time dairies with Khmer men and women, it quickly became apparent that this could not be the true explanation. Women clearly had a great deal less leisure time and far longer working hours than men.[2] In the absence of a clear difference in available time, the obvious conclusion is that Khmer women prioritise their time differently because they attach a greater importance to attending public meetings. This was confirmed in one of the focus group discussions, when the women said they were interested in meetings because they could see the benefits to themselves and the ways attendance could "improve their lives". In subsequent discussion, it emerged that one of these benefits was that "their opinions would be listened to". On the other hand,

---

[2] This result is in accordance with World Bank research which shows that, in Vietnam, women generally have much longer working hours than men (World Bank, 1999).

Poverty: Malaise of Development

they felt that women were not important decision-makers at a community level. While women often attend meetings, they do not participate in the same way as men. Women not only have difficulty in participating because of a perceived lack of knowledge, language skills and education, but also because taking an active role in public meetings runs counter to the popular moral image of how a woman should behave. In the words of a middle-aged Khmer man from Soc Trang: "The men are more active in the meetings. It's because a man is stronger than a woman; he can speak more clearly and express himself better." Women often mentioned "being shy" as a reason to stay quiet in meetings.

Although it was observed that many women attend meetings, women-only focus groups revealed that it is still not uncommon for men to restrict their wives' participation in out-of-house activities, such as participation in the Women's Union. The difficulties Khmer women experience in participating in meetings are significant, as heavily segregated gender roles also determine what topics men view as "men's issues" or "women's issues". In one of the focus groups, which comprised Khmer men only, women's health, family planning and sanitation were identified as "topics for women". In the women's focus groups, women agreed with this. As a middle-aged woman from Soc Trang province put it: "Men know more about farming; a woman only knows about housework." In fact, women compare well to men in relation to being informed. In many focus group discussions, women mentioned watching news programmes on television and discussing news amongst themselves. In spite of this, both men and women often expressed the perception that women do not know as much as men. The gender aspect of the participation problem is doubly significant, because Khmer people typically live in areas characterised by poor sanitation, lack of clean drinking water and lack of access to health care, which contribute to higher rates of infant mortality and adult illness. As all of these concerns are culturally labelled as "women's problems", it is essential that women have the ability to both attend and understand meetings. In fact, the Mekong River Regional Poverty Assessment lists long-term illness as one of the most important reasons for households to fall into poverty (UNDP & AusAID, 2004).

The focus group discussions show that Khmer people suffer from a combination of factors that effectively limit their ability to access essential sources of information and to make use of the main channel through which they can inform policy. Language, lack of confidence and segregated gender roles result in an inability to understand and participate in what goes on in village meetings. Better education would remove some, if not all, of these barriers, but the education system is not structured in a way that makes it likely that Khmer pupils will succeed. As a consequence, a lack of access to essential information may continue through the generations. However, when economic reform requires greater knowledge and flexibility, this lack of access to information becomes much more significant.

Intangible assets and economic outcomes

As discussed in earlier sections, the last decade has seen rising levels of inequality both between and within provinces. The Mekong Delta is no exception to this trend. Research by AusAID (2004) shows that, in the Mekong Delta, those most at risk of being poor are people who are landless, people who live in rural areas, Khmer ethnic minorities, women and particularly people who fit more than one of the aforementioned categories. Typically, the

Poverty: Malaise of Development

Khmer people fit into most of the risk categories listed. The majority of the Khmer people live in remote rural areas, typically furthest from the road network. While Kinh famers in the Mekong Delta normally have two or three crops a year, Khmer households normally have only one low-yield rice crop per year, because of poor quality soil and lack of irrigation (Food Security and Agricultural Projects Analysis Service, 2004).

These conditions, already problematic, are worsening. In the last decade, the Khmer people have lost their agricultural lands at an unprecedented rate. There are two major reasons for the growing landlessness among the Khmer people in the delta. First of all, the Khmer people are frequently the victims of unfair land transactions, as their lack of knowledge and information makes them highly vulnerable to deception. One way in which this vulnerability can lead to land loss is through infrastructure projects.

In the last decade, the Vietnamese government has drastically improved the density and quality of the road network. In a government programme known as "Program 135", block grants were given to the district or commune people's committees in roughly 2,000 of Vietnam's poorest locations, together making up about 20% of Vietnam. The money came from American Development Aid funds. Communes were instructed to consult the community, for instance through village meetings, in order to identify which projects were needed to improve community-based infrastructure (Fritzen, 2005). Between 2000 and 2006, the World Bank funded an additional 1,800 new roads in 40 provinces in Vietnam (Minh, 2007). Though the World Bank had claimed that there has been no corruption in the building of roads (Minh, 2007), the majority opinion is that a substantial amount of money from these projects was diverted, an opinion which was shared by some

Ethnicity, Poverty and Trade Liberalisation

researchers working for the World Bank (Fritzen, 2005; Mu & Van de Walle, 2007). In my own fieldwork, I was more than once told by local people that corruption in road building projects was a fact of life.

Increasing levels of corruption are a by-product of the decentralisation that has accompanied the shift from a planned economy to a market one. In the planned economy, local government was dependent on the central government for the allocation of resources. Reform has given commune and district people's committees greater control of expenditure, and many local governments have shares in local companies or own companies themselves. Such private-public relationships can be profitable to both – the companies have advance knowledge of regulations and can negotiate preferential treatment, whereas the local government can generate greater income. In short, the greater amount of money and the greater power of local government has increased both the scope for corruption and the amount of money involved (Gainsborough, 2003).

However, unequal benefits can arise purely out of unequal distribution of knowledge rather than money. In various publications, Taylor describes how infrastructure projects give rise to speculation in land by those with advance knowledge of the projects, at the expense of those who are unaware that infrastructure projects are being planned. In this way, the main beneficiaries of road development have been people who bought land at very cheap prices, either in order subsequently to get higher compensation after roads were built or to set up businesses near newly built roads. As a consequence, Khmer people are driven further away from transport networks into more remote areas (Taylor, 2004b; 2007; 2008). He quotes a local shopkeeper who openly discusses the effect this speculation has on the Khmer minority people: "the way to get rich quickest is to buy land from Khmer people who ...

Poverty: Malaise of Development

do not understand the ways of the world [and] sell up quickly at a fraction of the land's true cost". Taylor showed that both government officials and the local Kinh people make use of the Khmer people's lack of knowledge as a way to obtain valuable land cheaply (Taylor, 2004b).

The effect of infrastructure projects on the Khmer ethnic minorities is important, as many such projects were undertaken with the aim of reducing ethnic minority poverty by connecting the areas in which they live to markets, as a lack of access to markets is often regarded as a major contributor to ethnic minority poverty (Rerkasem, 2003). The mechanism of landlessness underscores the importance of access to village meetings. One of the reasons Khmer people lack knowledge about the infrastructure projects planned in their area is that they do not receive the information provided in village meetings, where infrastructure plans are discussed. Moreover, Khmer people's lack of Vietnamese restricts their ability to create personal networks outside their own community, separating them from informal sources of information.

Another way by which people lose their land is through adverse shocks, when farmers are forced to sell land in the face of a serious and immediate lack of money. The reasons for lack of profits from farming are twofold. On the one hand, in an environment of increasing competition, farms need to become more efficient. Rural incomes are therefore likely to depend on the most profitable use of the land. As discussed in the previous section, Khmer people have very restricted access to information when it is delivered in Vietnamese, resulting in a lack of knowledge about irrigation methods, types of crops, crop diseases, pests, etc. Like other ethnic minorities, Khmer people have very limited access to the technical knowledge that they need to make their farming more efficient. Secondly, farmers who augment income through off-farm rural employment are far less sensitive to adverse shocks, as they have an alternative source of income. Employment opportunities, however, are much more limited for people with little or no education. In a sample of 150 Kinh farmers I interviewed in An Giang, the vast majority of households had members who worked in regular occupations, including tailors, government officials, factory workers, nurses and teachers. Uneducated farmers typically work on other people's land, a source of income which is seasonal and irregular. The two most important factors determining the ability to find regular and well-paid off-farm employment are education and close connections with public servants (UNDP & AusAid, 2004). Again, these are typically the two advantages that Khmer people do not have.

While selling land may offer some immediate relief to poor farmers, the long-term effect of land sale is likely to be a further descent into poverty. In the Mekong Delta, poverty and landlessness are strongly associated characteristics (Ravallion & Van de Walle, 2008). The increasing landlessness among ethnic majorities in the Mekong Delta is therefore a serious cause for concern.

While the preceding paragraphs show that trade reform policies can have negative effects on the Khmer communities, the main reason for the increasing poverty divide is not that trade liberalisation harms Khmer people directly. The poverty levels experienced by the Khmer communities have become slightly less severe over the past decade, but development gains made by the Kinh majority people have far outstripped improvements among the Khmer. As long as the Khmer people remain isolated from Vietnamese society, they will be unable to make the adjustments to their livelihoods that would allow them to prosper during trade reform. The key to solving the ethnic minority poverty divide is therefore to close the particular social divide that handicaps the Khmer people when they try to access education, knowledge and networks.

Conclusion

Whilst Vietnam is becoming increasingly integrated into the global economic community, Vietnam's Khmer minority people are excluded from many of the resulting benefits. Public discourse often links the Khmer people's poverty to their culture, religion and customs. However, people do not need to become less Khmer to become less poor. This chapter has shown that it is not their difference in itself that keeps people from escaping poverty, but the isolating effects that differences in culture and language produce.

To tackle efficiently this ethnic poverty divide will require the government to make an ideological shift, from focusing on the security risks posed by the Khmer people to a focus on the mobilisation of the Khmer people's potential to improve their lives. Focus group discussions demonstrated the strategic importance of involving women in the development of Khmer communities. In focus group discussions, women showed they were highly motivated in finding ways to improve their lives. At the local level, village meetings provide a good setting to discuss development needs. However, to participate successfully in these meetings, the Khmer people, especially the women, need to have sufficient confidence and skill.

In the short run, some of the barriers to access and information could be lowered by increasing the number of translators available at all public meetings, and by providing more resources in the Khmer language. In the long run, better access to education is the most essential route out of poverty. Khmer-language tuition, currently restricted by law, and more support for students who are non-native speakers of Vietnamese, would help to boost the performance of Khmer students. However, greater achievements could be made if a way could be found to tackle the stereotyping of the Khmer and the Kinh people. The popular media could feature ethnic minority customs as qualities that enrich Vietnam's diverse culture. Community projects could be used to improve dialogues between Khmer and Kinh people, and to help break down preconceived images of the "otherness" of these ethnic groups.

Trade liberalisation has made the integration of the Khmer minority people more urgent, as the adjustments required by trade liberalisation put greater pressures on people with fewer assets. It has also created better conditions for their exploitation by those with greater market strength. On the other hand, Vietnam's increased exposure to international scrutiny has also created new opportunities for the Khmer Krom people to make their voices heard. Khmer Krom groups have successfully used the internet to create virtual networks with English-language information, such as the Khmer Kampuchea Krom Federation [KKF] and the Khmer Krom Network. Moreover, Khmer minority problems have now drawn the attention of international organisations such as Amnesty International, Human Rights Watch and the Unrepresented Nations and Peoples Organisation [UNPO]. Hopefully, the Vietnamese government will respond to this international pressure by finding a new, more inclusive approach to deal with the ethnic minority people living within its borders.

References

AusAID. (2004). *Mekong Delta poverty analysis*. Canberra: Australian Agency for International Development.

Ba, H. T., Hanh, D. B., & Cuong, B. T. (2002). *Indigenous peoples/ethnic minorities and poverty reduction: Vietnam*. Manila: Asian Development Bank.

Baulch, B., Chuyen, T. T. K., Haughton, D., & Haughton, J. (2002). Ethnic minority development in Vietnam: A socioeconomic perspective. In P. Glewwe, N. Agrawal, & D. Dollar (Eds.), *Economic growth, poverty, and household welfare in Vietnam* (pp. 273-310). Washington, DC: World Bank.

Baulch, B., Chuyen, T. T. K., Haughton, D., & Haughton, J. (2007). Ethnic minority development in Vietnam. *Journal of Development Studies, 43* (7), 1151-76.

Baulch, B., & Masset, E. (2003). Do monetary and nonmonetary indicators tell the same story about chronic poverty?: A study of Vietnam in the 1990s. *World Development, 31* (3), 441-53.

Beresford, M. (2003). Economic transition, uneven development, and the impact of reform. In H. V. Luong (Ed.), *Postwar Vietnam: Dynamics of a transforming society*. Singapore: Rowman and Littlefield.

Ethnicity, Poverty and Trade Liberalisation

Binh, N. N., & Haughton, J. (2002). Trade liberalization and foreign direct investment in Vietnam. *ASEAN Economic Bulletin, 19* (3), 302-18.

Chambers, R., & Conway, G. R. (1992). *Sustainable rural livelihoods: Practical concepts for the 21st century.* Brighton: Institute of Development Studies.

Clayton, T. (2006). The shape of hegemony: Vietnam in Cambodia, 1979-1989. In T. Clayton (Ed.), *Rethinking hegemony.* Albert Park, Victoria: James Nicholas.

Coe, M. D., & Cof, M. D. (1957). The Khmer settlement pattern: A possible analogy with that of the Maya. *American Antiquity, 22* (4), 409-10.

Food Security and Agricultural Projects Analysis Service. (2004). *Food insecurity and vulnerability in Viet Nam: Profiles of four vulnerable groups.* Rome: Food and Agriculture Organization of the United Nations, Agricultural and Development Economics Division.

Fritzen, S. (2002). Growth, inequality and the future of poverty reduction in Vietnam. *Journal of Asian Economics, 13* (5), 635-57.

Fritzen, S. (2005). The 'misery' of implementation: Governance, institutions and anti-corruption in

Vietnam. In N. Tarling (Ed.), *Corruption and good governance in Asia* (pp. 98-120). London: Routledge.

Gainsborough, M. (2003). Corruption and the politics of economic decentralisation in Vietnam. *Journal of Contemporary Asia, 33*(1), 69-84.

Heo, Y., & Doanh, N. K. (2009). Trade liberalisation and poverty reduction in Vietnam. *World Economy, 32* (6), 934-64.

Hertel, T. W. (2006). A survey of findings on the poverty impacts of agricultural trade liberalization. *Electronic Journal of Agricultural and Development Economics, 3* (1), 1-26.

Human Rights Watch. (2009). *On the margins: Rights abuses of ethnic Khmer in Vietnam's Mekong Delta.* New York: Author.

Jensen, H. T., & Tarp, F. (2005). Trade liberalization and spatial inequality: A methodological innovation in a Vietnamese perspective. *Review of Development Economics, 9* (1), 69-86.

Justino, P., & Litchfield, J. (2002). *Poverty dynamics in rural Vietnam: Winners and losers during reform.* Brighton: University of Sussex, Poverty Research Unit at Sussex.

Kabeer, N., & Van Anh, T. T. (2006). *Globalisation, gender and work in the context of economic transition: The case of Vietnam.* Salt Lake City, UT: GEM-IWG (International Working Group on Gender, Macroeconomics, and International Economics).

Mattner, M. (2004). Power to the people?: Local governance and politics in Vietnam. *Environment and Urbanization, 16* (1), 121-128.

McElwee, P. (2004). Becoming socialist or becoming Kinh: Government policies for ethnic minorities in the Socialist Republic of Vietnam. In C. R. Duncan (Ed.), *Civilizing the margins: Southeast Asian government policies for the development of minorities* (pp. 241-69). Ithaca, NY: Cornell University Press.

Minh, H. B. (2007, May 28). World Bank says no corruption in Vietnam road projects. *Reuters AlertNet.* Retrieved July 6, 2009, from: http://www.alertnet.org/thenews/newsdesk/HAN198101.htm

Mu, R., & Van de Walle, D. (2007). *Rural roads and poor area development in Vietnam.* Washington, DC: World Bank.

Nguyen Ngoc, D. (2006). *Farmers, agriculture and rural development in the Mekong Delta of Vietnam.* Ho Chi Minh City: Education Publishing House.

Nguyen, T., Le, D. T., Vu, H. D., & Nguyen, T. P. (2006). *Poverty, poverty reduction and poverty dynamics in Vietnam.* Manchester: Chronic Poverty Research Centre.

Nguyen, T. D., & Ezaki, M. (2005). Regional economic integration and its impacts on growth, poverty and income distribution: The case of Vietnam. *Review of Urban and Regional Development Economics, 17* (3), 117-215.

Nguyen, V. P. (2009). *What education for the ethnic minorities of Vietnam?: Pre-schooling as a pattern of social integration.* Bangkok: UNESCO Bangkok.

Ovesen, J., & Trankell, I.-B. (2004). Foreigners and honorary Khmers. In C. R. Duncan (Ed.), *Civilizing the margins: Southeast Asian government policies for the development of minorities* (pp. 241-269). Ithaca, NY: Cornell University Press.

Peang-Meth, A. (1991). Understanding the Khmer: Sociological-cultural observations. *Asian Survey, 31* (5), 442-55.

Pelley, P. (1998). "Barbarians" and "younger brothers": The remaking of race in postcolonial Vietnam. *Journal of Southeast Asian Studies, 29* (2), 347-91.

Ravallion, M., & Van de Walle, D. (2008). Does rising landlessness signal success or failure for Vietnam's agrarian transition? *Journal of Development Economics, 87* (2), 191-209.

Reardon, T., Stamoulis, K., & Pingali, P. (2007). Rural nonfarm employment in developing countries in an era of globalization. *Agricultural Economics, 37* (S1), 173-83.

Rerkasem, K. (2003). Uplands land use. In M. Kaosa-ard & J. Dore (Eds.), *Social challenges for the Mekong region* (pp. 323-46). Bangkok: White Lotus.

Scott, S., & Lloyd, F. M. K. (2006). Doing fieldwork in development geography: Research culture and research spaces in Vietnam. *Geographical Research, 44* (1), 28-40.

SOS: Pupils dropping like flies in Cuu Long River Delta. (2009, March 17). *Vietnamnet Bridge.* Retrieved July 20, 2009, from: http://english.vietnamnet.vn/education/2008/03/773791/

Taylor, P. (2004a). Introduction: Social inequality in a socialist state. In P. Taylor (Ed.), *Social inequality in*

Poverty: Malaise of Development *Vietnam and the challenges to reform* (pp. 1-40). Singapore: Institute of Southeast Asian Studies.

Taylor, P. (2004b). Redressing disadvantage or re-arranging inequality?: Development interventions and local responses in the Mekong Delta. In P. Taylor (Ed.), *Social inequality in Vietnam and the challenges to reform* (pp. 236-69). Singapore: Institute of Southeast Asian Studies.

Taylor, P. (2007). Poor policies, wealthy peasants: Alternative trajectories of rural development in Vietnam. *Journal of Vietnamese Studies, 2* (2), 3-56.

Taylor, P. (2008). Minorities at large: New approaches to minority ethnicity in Vietnam. *Journal of Vietnamese Studies, 3* (3), 3-43.

Tinh, V. X. (2001, February-March). *Changing land policies and its impacts on land tenure of ethnic minorities in Vietnam*. Paper presented at the Eighth Workshop on Community Management of Forest Lands, East-West Center, Honolulu.

UNDP, & AusAID. (2004). *The regional poverty assessment: Mekong River region, 2003*. Hanoi. Authors.

Van, D. N., Son, C. T., & Hung, L. (2000). *Ethnic minorities in Vietnam*. Hanoi: Thê Giói Publishers.

Ethnicity, Poverty and Trade Liberalisation

Van de Walle, D., & Gunewardena, D. (2001). Sources of ethnic inequality in Viet Nam. *Journal of Development Economics, 65* (1), 177-207.

Vietnam rejects false report on Khmer ethnic people. (2009, January 27). *Nhân Dân*. Retrieved July 20, 2009, from: http://nhandan.com.vn/english/news/270109/domestic_vietnam.htm

Vietnam rejects Human Rights Watch's fabrication. (2009, January 24). *VOVNews*. Retrieved July 20, 2009, from: http://english.vovnews.vn/Home/Vietnam-rejects-Human-Rights-Watchs-fabrication/20091/101371.vov

Winters, L. A., McCulloch, N., & McKay, A. (2004). Trade liberalization and poverty: The evidence so far. *Journal of Economic Literature, 42* (1), 72-115.

World Bank. (1999). *Vietnam development report 2000: Attacking poverty*. Hanoi: Author.

World Bank. (2003). *Vietnam development report 2004: Poverty*. Hanoi: Author.

FAITH MATTERS: DEVELOPMENT AND THE COMPLEX WORLD OF FAITH-BASED ORGANISATIONS[1]

Gerard Clarke

1. Introduction

In recent years, religion and faith have assumed a more important place in development discourse and policy.[2] A key factor has been the growth of faith-based activism around the cause of international development, illustrated in particular by the Jubilee 2000 campaign. Founded in 1996, Jubilee 2000 originated in earlier plans to link demands for debt relief to the old Jewish (and later, Christian) concept of *jubilee*, a year in every fifty in which creditors forgive debtors, slaves are set free and forfeited land is returned to its original owners, restoring harmony to a turbulent socio-economic order.[3] Beginning in the UK, the campaign mobilised local church congregations through faith-based activities highlighting the problem of developing country debt. In the late 1990s, Jubilee 2000 had

---

[1]This chapter is partly based on research undertaken in 2004-5 by the Centre for Development Studies, Swansea, and the Department of Theology and Religious Studies, University of Wales Lampeter, on behalf of the Department for International Development, focusing on DFID engagement with FBOs and the role of faith groups in poverty reduction. I am grateful in particular to Ian Linden, Dawoud El-Alami, Maya Warrier, Jim Manor and Mohammed Kroessin for helpful advice or comments. I bear full responsibility, however, for mistakes or omissions here.
[2] See Clarke (2006) for a more detailed examination of the convergence of faith and development.
[3] "This fiftieth year you shall make sacred by proclaiming liberty in the land for all its inhabitants. It shall be a jubilee for you ..." (Lev. 25:10 [New American Bible]).

affiliates in more than 60 countries, and by 1999 had collected 24 million signatures, the largest global petition in history. With other NGOs and networks, Jubilee 2000 mobilised nearly 60,000 demonstrators at the 1999 G7 meeting in Cologne.[4] According to J. D. Clark:

> Jubilee 2000, on a shoestring budget, probably contributed more to poor countries financially than all operational NGOs [non-governmental organisations] combined by wresting for them up to $100 billion of debt relief from unwilling G7 governments and IGOs [intergovernmental organisations] and by ensuring that much of this was redistributed to basic services in those countries. (J. D. Clark, 2003, p. 137)

Jubilee 2000 made a big impression on British political leaders. Chancellor of the Exchequer Gordon Brown, for instance, described it as the most significant social movement in Britain since John Wesley (the Christian theologian and founder of Methodism) led the eighteenth-century campaign against slavery with the parliamentarian William Wilberforce (cf. Wallis, 2005, pp. xvi, 272). The former Secretary of State for International Development, Clare Short, was equally impressed and appealed to faith communities in 2002 to join the campaign in support of the Millennium Declaration agreed at the United Nations General Assembly in 2000 and the associated Millennium Development Goals [MDGs]:[5]

---

[4] See Collins, Gariyo & Burdon, (2001) or Marshall & Keough, (2004) for further details.
[5] For the full text of the Millennium Declaration, see www.un.org/millennium/summit.htm. For details of the MDGs, see www.un.org/millenniumgoals/index.html.

Poverty: Malaise of Development

> Faith groups have an important role to play [in the achievement of the MDGs].... We need to mobilise that core of moral teaching that lies at the heart of each of the world's great religions: that life must be just and fair and that all human beings deserve respect and opportunity to enjoy their humanity and practise their spirituality. We need to mobilise faith organisations in our communities to catalyze public opinions and to sensitize populations to our duty to care for the world's poor, to shift global economic rules, to reshape global institutions and to make aid available at required levels. (Short, 2003, pp. 8-9)

Short's argument draws attention to the complex world of Faith-based Organisations [FBOs]. Many types of organisations fall under the rubric of "faith organisations" as conceived by Short and such organisations use and deploy faith in different ways in the context of "development" in national and international settings. This complexity, however, remains poorly understood among development policy-makers and practitioners, many of whom remain wedded to a predominantly secular view of development. Western European donors, for instance, have traditionally supported the work of relief and development organisations supported by the mainstream Christian organisations, but have missed opportunities for engagement with other types of organisation because of fears of blurring established church-state boundaries or of supporting sectarian or chauvinistic agendas. With this problem in mind, Section 2 below presents a typology of FBOs and examines the ways in which different types of FBO contribute to development. Section 3 analyses the ways in which such organisations use faith discourse in the context of development debates and development policy, and looks at some of the operational challenges that arise. Section 4, the conclusion, considers implications that result for donors, development NGOs and other actors eager to understand and engage with FBOs in the context of international development.

2. The complex world of faith-based organisations

FBOs are a complex set of actors in development contexts because they come in a variety of organisational guises and have differential effects (both positive and negative) in the context of international development. The key world religions, for instance, subdivide into different branches and the ethos of a FBO may derive from one of these. Christianity comes in three main forms (Catholic, Protestant and Orthodox/Coptic), yet each can be further sub-divided (Protestant churches, for instance can be mainstream or evangelical). Islam divides into the Sunni and Shia traditions, yet further subdivides into a variety of derivative traditions, depending on allegiance to the teachings of a prophet or an ethno-national grouping: for instance, Hanafi, Hambali, Maliki, Sufi, Salafi, Wahabi, Ahmadi, or Ismaili. Hinduism, meanwhile, is a diverse religion that includes major traditions such as Vaishnavism, Shivaism and Shaktism, but also hundreds of minor traditions, often confined to a specific locality. Similar distinctions can be made between faith/sub-faith systems and associated FBOs on the basis of their commitment to social engagement, their support of the poor or their compatibility with contemporary development discourse. Liberation theology (in the case of Catholicism), the prosperity gospel (in the case of Christian evangelism), socially-engaged Buddhism and civil Islam, for instance, share important similarities with development discourse, while mainstream Catholicism, *Hindutva*

Poverty: Malaise of Development

(sectarian Hindu nationalism), fundamental Buddhism, or Wahabism (in the case of Islam) run counter to it in significant respects.

Clearly then, there are many ways to cut the cake, in so far as FBOs as a set of organisations are concerned. Here, the focus is on organisations involved in:

1. Public policy debates and associated political contests concerned with national and international development;
2. Social and political processes that impact positively or negatively on the poor; and
3. Direct efforts to support, represent, or engage with, the poor.

In this context, five types of FBO are evident:

Faith-based representative organisations or apex bodies, which rule on doctrinal matters, govern the faithful and represent them through engagement with the state and other actors;

Faith-based charitable or development organisations, which mobilise the faithful in support of the poor and other social groups, and which fund or manage programmes which tackle poverty and social exclusion;

Faith-based socio-political organisations, which interpret and deploy faith as a political construct, organising and mobilising social groups on the basis of faith identities, but in pursuit of broader political objectives; or, alternatively, promote faith as a socio-cultural construct, as a means of uniting disparate social groups on the basis of faith-based cultural identities;

Faith Matters

Faith-based missionary organisations, which spread key faith messages beyond the faithful by actively promoting the faith and seeking converts to it, or by supporting and engaging with other faith communities on the basis of key faith principles;
And finally, *faith-based radical, illegal or terrorist organisations,* which promote radical or militant forms of faith identity, engage in illegal practices on the basis of faith beliefs, or engage in armed struggle or violent acts, justified on the grounds of faith.

This five-fold typology captures a wide variety of organisational forms and an equally varied range of impacts in development contexts. *Faith-based representative organisations or apex bodies,* for instance, vary across the main religions or faiths; the mainstream Christian Churches (Catholic, Protestant and Orthodox/Coptic), are hierarchically-organised, so representative bodies have an official status and are usually unchallenged by rival organisations, allowing them to speak with authority to the faithful and to represent them in engagement with other stakeholders. Similarly, in national settings, Buddhism is usually characterised by a central and legitimate authority, the *sangha* (the monastic community of monks, nuns and novices). Other key religions, however, are less hierarchically organised. Islam, for instance, is based on significant devolution of religious and political authority and no single organisation represents the Muslim faith globally.[6] Similarly, Hinduism represents a diverse tradition that lacks a single founder, creed or moral system and therefore lacks a coherent political or administrative

---

[6] Although the Saudi-sponsored World Muslim League enjoys some support among Sunni Muslims.

structure in national or international settings. The absence of representative organisations with a broad-based legitimacy among adherents to non-Christian traditions, therefore, militates against the global mobilisation of the faithful in support of international development. It also prevents donors from identifying obvious representative interlocutors. However, the need to mobilise the world's faith communities in the battle against global poverty makes it critical that donors should work with faith communities to identify such interlocutors and involve them in multilateral forums.

Representative organisations or apex bodies often include subsidiary organisations which promote development or charitable work, but otherwise they remained aloof from international development debates until comparatively recently. In recent years, such organisations have become more involved in international dialogues concerned with poverty reduction, debt relief and the global fight against HIV/AIDS. Leaders of international organisations such as the World Council of Churches [WCC] or national organisations, such as the United States Conference of Catholic Bishops [USCCB], were active in the Jubilee 2000 campaign and in the more recent global campaign to "Make Poverty History". These processes, and the involvement of such organisations and leaders which they sustain, are critical to the global fight against poverty because they represent and mobilise constituencies traditionally estranged by purely secular development discourse.

The second category, *faith-based charitable or development organisations*, play a more direct role in tackling poverty and inequality by funding or managing programmes that help the poor and by raising awareness of poverty among the faithful. In the industrialised "North", FBOs play an important role in providing social services to the poor. In

Faith Matters

the USA, for instance, an estimated 18% of the 37,000 non-profit organisations involved in social service provision in 1999 had a faith-based ethos (Wuthnow, 2004, p. 141). These FBOs had estimated assets of $25.5 billion and annual budgets of $17 billion in 1999, equivalent to the annual gross national income [GNI] of medium-sized economies such as Syria, Sri Lanka or Costa Rica.[7] FBOs, clearly, have significant economic, as well as political, muscle.

Faith-based social engagement at home is mirrored in support for the poor in developing countries. Members of the *Coopération Internationale pour le Développement et la Solidarité* [CIDSE] (or International Cooperation for Development and Solidarity), the largest alliance of Catholic development agencies, had a combined budget of $950 million in 2000; members of the Association of Protestant Development [APRODEV], the main association of Protestant development agencies, had $470 million; and World Vision International [WVI], the single largest Christian development agency, had turnover of $600 million in 1999 (Clark, J. D., 2003, pp. 134-6). Including Caritas International, the second main international coalition of Catholic development agencies, the big four faith-based development agencies (CIDSE, World Vision, APRODEV and Caritas) had a combined annual income of approximately $2.5 billion at the beginning of the new millennium, or almost two thirds of the annual budget of the UK Department for International Development [DFID]

---

[7] The 37,000 NPOs [Non-profit Organisations] had assets of approximately $142 billion and annual budgets of $93 billion in 1999 (Wuthnow, 2004, pp. 140 & 325, n.5). This estimate assumes that FBOs have proportionately similar resources to all NPOs (Wuthnow, p. 142). In 2002, Syria, Sri Lanka and Costa Rica had Gross National Income [GNI] of US$19 billion., 16 billion and 16 billion respectively (http://www.worldbank.org/data/dataquery.html).

Poverty: Malaise of Development

(£2.7 billion, or $4 billion in 2000/2001).[8] As such, they have become significant players in the international delivery of aid, the equivalent of large bilateral donors, although this power is more latent than manifest, partly because of a twin antipathy to non-governmental actors and to faith-based organisations on the part of governmental donors.

Faith-based development and charitable organisations have become equally prevalent and significant in developing countries. Across the Arab world, for instance, Islamic charitable organisations proliferated during the 1990s as a result of political reform and economic liberalisation (in most cases), or state fragility or collapse (in a minority of cases, such as Palestine or Somalia). In Egypt, an estimated 20% of the 12,832 registered voluntary organisations in 1997 were Islamic in character (Clark, J. A., 2004, p. 12). According to World Bank research, Islamic NGOs in Egypt are less dependent on state aid than secular NGOs and better able to raise funds locally (Clark, J. A., 2004, pp. 60-61). In Somalia, Islamic NGOs have played an important role in providing social services in the absence of an effective state. Almost all schools, for instance, are privately run and Islamic NGOs have played a vital role in channelling Arab funding to them (NOVIB [Oxfam Netherlands] & World Assembly of Muslim Youth, 2004).

The third category, *faith-based socio-political organisations*, is the most diverse, and includes political parties, broad-based social movements, cultural organisations and secret societies. They differ from representative organisations and apex bodies in that they do not normally claim to rule on doctrinal matters or to govern the faithful. Instead, they interpret and deploy faith as a political construct, organising and mobilising social

---

[8] DFID figures: Department for International Development, 2001.

Faith Matters

groups on the basis of faith identities in pursuit of broader political objectives or, alternatively, they promote faith as a socio-cultural construct, as a means of uniting disparate social groups on the basis of faith-based cultural identities. Such organisations have become increasingly important amid the rise of identity politics as a driver of change in national and international contexts (cf. Clarke, 2006).

Throughout the world, for instance, many political parties have a faith-based ethos. Christian democracy, for example, originated as a political ideology in the late nineteenth century when Pope Leo XIII's papal encyclical *Rerum Novarum* acknowledged the suffering of workers and the role of Christian compassion in combating it. Today, Christian democratic parties are active throughout Europe and also Australia, Chile and Namibia. Islam has been equally adapted to political purposes and faith-based political parties are common throughout the Islamic world, including the *Muttahaida Majlis-I-Amal* [MMA], a coalition of six political parties in Pakistan which secured 11.3% of the vote in parliamentary elections in 2002.[9] In Indonesia, the world's largest predominantly Muslim country, Islamic parties garnered 16% of the vote in the 1999 general elections, support which they have retained in subsequent elections and opinion polls.[10] Faith-based political parties draw significant support from sections of the poor and are therefore important stakeholders in the framing of national strategies to reduce poverty. Overseas donors, therefore, face challenges in engaging with the discourses of such parties and developing constructive forms of engagement.

---

[9] On the MMA's electoral performance, see *Europa World Yearbook 2004*, Vol. 2, p. 3263.
[10] See 'Terrorism Undermines Political Islam in Indonesia', YaleGlobal online (www.yaleglobal.yale.edu), 26 November 2003.

Poverty: Malaise of Development

Islamic political parties have been central to the rise of political Islam as a potent force in national and international politics, but broad-based social movements have, arguably, played a greater role. Political Islam is most closely associated with the Muslim Brotherhood, founded by Hassan El Banna in Egypt in 1928, which has branches today in over 70 countries and a membership of many millions, mostly in the Arab world. In a number of Arab states, it has been associated with armed struggles against colonial rule or against the nationalist, but secular, regimes which replaced it. It also functions, however, as a pan-Arab and pan-Islamic social movement, which feeds on middle-class resentment at arbitrary state rule and the perceived humiliation of the *ummah* (the community of Muslims) at the hands of Western powers, and plays an important role in the organisation and delivery of social services to the Muslim poor. A controversial force across the Islamic world, the Brotherhood is attacked for promoting terrorism and exclusive political identities in multi-ethnic and multi-religious societies, yet respected for its social activism and its support (sometimes tactical) for multi-party democracy.[11]

Political Islam is largely concerned with restoring Islam as the organising principle of political power and social order, and the political basis of both the nation state and the pan-national *ummah*. As such, it challenges ruling secular political parties, perceived to have marginalised Islam from political life. Moderate political Islam promotes the gradual Islamisation of the nation state and concedes that the Islamist project must make tactical concessions in pursuit of its strategy. It promotes Islam as the answer to the social, economic and political ills that afflict Muslim

---

[11] For summary details, see Kepel, (2001) or, for country-specific studies, see Wiktorowicz, (2001) on Jordan or Mishal & Sela, (2000) on Palestine.

societies, arguing effectively that it is the solution (or at least that it frames the solutions), to development dilemmas across the Islamic world. According to Janine Clark, it is best understood as a reaction against state encroachment on religious authority, including the takeover of mosque-based social services by the state (Clark, J. A., 2004, p. 12). In some respects, therefore, moderate political Islam represents the struggle for autonomous civil societies in Muslim countries, where the secular state exists alongside an active community of Islamic FBOs, some of which accept the legitimacy of the state, while others challenge it. This provides a potential basis for donors to engage in social movements, otherwise viewed as opposed to the mainstream development enterprise.

Political parties and social movements are important because of their overt role in mobilising social groups on the basis of faith and other identities, but secret societies with an explicit faith ethos can have an equivalent influence on the design and implementation of public policy through covert networking among elite social groups. In the West, for instance, the Freemasons derive members primarily from mainstream Protestantism and have exercised a shadowy, often corrupt, influence on the functioning of public institutions, including the judiciary and police, while Opus Dei, the secretive Catholic sect, has been accused of supporting right-wing and fascist regimes during the 1970s. In sub-Saharan Africa, political networks are often based on a common allegiance to secret societies that blend mainstream Christianity and traditional African beliefs. Here, according to Ellis & Haar (2004, p. 78), secret societies of European origin sit easily with indigenous traditions of closed societies, especially in former French colonies influenced by French traditions of freemasonry. "A key attraction of secret societies", they write, "is that

Poverty: Malaise of Development

membership provides opportunities for doing deals unobserved by the mass of the population and for forming bonds of solidarity that go beyond the ordinary", based on a widespread belief in the omnipresence of spiritual power (Ellis & Haar, p. 83). Secret societies, however, represent an element of civil society which liberal discourse and donor policy have traditionally ignored. Supporting "good governance", fighting corruption and expanding the scope of civil society in sub-Saharan Africa, however, depends in part on exposing the activities of such societies, encouraging them to evolve into formal and transparent organisations and supporting institutional alternatives, such as political parties or social movements, based on heterogeneous and public identities.

The fourth category considered here is *missionary organisations*, which have long been active in the context of international development, but never more so than today. Missionary organisations associated with the mainstream Christian churches are the forerunners of modern-day development NGOs in their commitment to the provision of social services and in their support of the local poor. Such organisations, however, have been eclipsed in recent decades by the proliferation of missionary organisations from other faith traditions. In the USA, for instance, the rise of the Christian right has led to a significant expansion in overseas missionary activity by evangelical and Pentecostal congregations.[12] In 2001, an estimated 350,000 Americans travelled abroad with Protestant missionary agencies, and donations to such agencies totalled $3.75 billion, a 44% increase in five years,[13] and significantly

---

[12] By the late 1980s, for instance, an estimated 90% of American Protestant missionaries were evangelicals (cf. Hearn, 2002, p. 39).

[13] Peter Waldman, 'Evangelicals Give U.S. Foreign Policy an Activist Tinge', *The Wall Street Journal*, 26 May 2004. See also Moreau (2000, p. 45) and Moreau, Corwin & McGee (2004, pp. 283 & 285) for equivalent

greater than the combined annual expenditure of the big four faith-based development NGO networks (CIDSE, APRODEV, Caritas and World Vision).[14] US evangelical missions in Africa, according to Hearn (2002, pp. 33-34), are critical to the implementation of donor, especially USAID, policy, yet effectively function as "invisible NGOs", because they have been ignored in the separate literatures on development NGOs and on African Christianity.

Similarly, the 1990s and early years of the new millennium have seen an increase in the number and reach of organisations committed to *tabligh wa-da'wa,* preaching the message of Allah *(da'wa,* or mission, for short) internationally. Throughout Africa, for instance, Arab organisations, including the World Muslim League (Saudi Arabia), the African Muslim Agency (Kuwait) and the World Islamic Call (Libya) fund local *madrasas* (Islamic seminaries or religious schools), promoting conservative Islamic currents such as Wahabism and Salafism, which traditionally have had little purchase in African societies. One significant consequence has been the emergence of a distinct cleavage in many countries between "African Islam", and "Islam in Africa", between traditional local forms of Islamic practice, and more conservative currents promoted by organisations from the Arab world.[15] Missionary activity characterised by active proselytising, however, is largely confined to Christianity and Islam. In India, some Hindu nationalist FBOs promote the

---

figures for 1996-1999. Moreau (2000), for instance, reports income of $2.93 billion in 1999.

[14] Although the figures for missionary organisations here include World Vision and other development NGOs associated with the US missionary tradition.

[15] See Rosander & Westerlund (1997) and Linden, Jawara & Pingle (2004).

reconversion of *adivasi* ("tribals") who convert from Hinduism to escape the oppressive social hierarchy of caste, but otherwise Hinduism lacks the tradition of seeking new converts to the faith, as do other major religions such as Buddhism and Sikhism. Evangelical Christian and Wahabi/Salafi organisations, therefore, represent a particular case for donors concerned to minimise potential for social conflict in complex cultural settings, yet equally concerned to reach constituencies traditionally disenfranchised by secular development discourse.

The fifth and final category, *faith-based radical, illegal or terrorist organisations*, have become important in development discourse and policy comparatively recently, largely as a result of the events of 9/11, and an emerging new nexus between security and development. Such groups typically grow out of two main political phenomena: *religious nationalism* (or communalism), directed against other religious communities; and *conservative religious politics* (or fundamentalism), directed mainly against secularists or enemies within the faith tradition (Keddie, 1998, p. 696). Such groups are common to all the major faith traditions, but Islam has been predominantly implicated in the promotion of faith-based violence and conflict in recent years. Loose international terrorist networks, such as *Al Qaeda* or *Jemaah Islamiyah*, promote a radical and puritanical vision of Islam. At heart, they seek the overthrow of the secular state across the Islamic world and the creation of a pan-national caliphate that unifies the world's Muslims under a single political and religious leader, serving as the direct successor of the Prophet Mohammed. This vision is both utopian and apocalyptic and few Muslims subscribe to it, yet, vulture-like, it feeds off a profound concern across the Islamic world at attacks on the *ummah* in multiple settings:

Faith Matters

Afghanistan, Bosnia, Chechnya, Iraq, Kashmir, Palestine, etc. From a development discourse and policy perspective, this concern is a real and significant obstacle to the broad-based, multi-stakeholder partnerships needed to promote international development in a world which is increasingly interlinked and interdependent.

In some settings, however, organisations with a propensity for violence are more socially embedded and represent a stronger case for conceptual and programmatic attention in the donor community. In the West Bank and Gaza Strip, for instance, Hamas[16] has emerged as a rival to the secular Fatah party as the principle representative of the Palestinian people. Hamas has achieved infamy in Israel and the West for indiscriminate suicide bombings, but is widely seen in Palestine, and by some academics, as a social movement that supports Palestinians in the absence of a viable state and government. Until 2005, when Saudi aid was reduced in support of the peace process, Hamas had an annual budget of approximately $70 million, 85% of which came from abroad. An estimated 90% of this budget, however, was spent on social services, including schools, health clinics and day-care centres;[17] a significant social safety net, given the weakness of the Palestinian Authority. The unexpected victory of Hamas in parliamentary elections in the West Bank and Gaza Strip, in January 2006, highlighted the challenge for Western donors posed by this dual character. In the short term, Western governments will cut aid to the Palestinian Authority, in the knowledge that Arab donors will make

---

[16] Literally 'Zeal' in Arabic, and the acronym for *Harakat al-Muqawama al-Islamiya* or Islamic Resistance Movement.

[17] 'Hamas, Islamic Jihad (Palestinian Islamists)', see Council on Foreign Relations, *Terrorism: Questions & Answers*, at: www.cfrterrorism.org/groups/hamas.html, which cites the Israeli scholar Reuvan Paz. On the social orientation of Hamas, see also Mishal & Sela, (2000, pp. 20-23).

Poverty: Malaise of Development

up the short fall; but in the medium term they face the challenge of engaging with Hamas (or at a minimum, its service provision arm) and both protecting and sustaining their investment in the construction of an embryonic Palestinian state.

3. The role of faith in the work of FBOs

FBOs are varied in their organisational guises, but they are also varied in the way they deploy faith in mobilising staff or supporters and in the way they work with beneficiaries and partners. As such they differ, to the extent that faith discourse provides the impulse for action, and that the goals for which they strive are rooted in the teachings and principles of the faith. This variation is important in development discourse and policy; multilateral, bilateral and non-governmental donors alike are wary of supporting organisations which seek advantage for the faith community, try to convert people, or attempt to advance one faith discourse at the expense of another. In some cases, it is illegal for them to do so but, more importantly, donors risk promoting conflict and social exclusion by supporting organisations that promote partisan agendas.

This makes it important to distinguish between the different uses of faith in the work of FBOs, a recent focus of academic research. In one study, Wuthnow reviews typologies of the role of faith in the work of US service provision FBOs, the most useful of which, Green and Sherman (2002), involves a study of 389 FBOs in 15 states participating in government-funded programmes (Wuthnow, 2004, pp. 142-9). The Green and Sherman study, with slight adaptations here, suggests a range of six possibilities, as follows:

Faith Matters

Not Relevant: The organization's faith commitments are not revealed, or are not evident, in its work with clients, beneficiaries or partners;

Passive: The organization's faith commitments are revealed through the act of caring for clients or supporting beneficiaries, rather than explicit mention of religious or spiritual matters;

Invitational: The organization's faith commitments are explicitly mentioned to clients, beneficiaries and partners, and they are invited to inquire more fully about religious or spiritual matters outside the programme;

Relational: The organization's faith commitments are explicitly mentioned to clients, beneficiaries and partners, and members of staff seek to establish personal relationships that involve religious or spiritual matters outside the programme;

Integrated: The organization's faith commitments are an explicit and critical part of its work with clients, beneficiaries and partners, but staff respect the rights of clients, etc., not to participate in the religious or spiritual aspects of a funded programme;

Mandatory: The organization's faith commitments are an explicit, critical and mandatory part of its work with clients, beneficiaries and partners who choose to participate in a programme or network.

Table 1, based on figures from Green and Sherman (2002), suggests that the majority of US service-provision FBOs do not see faith as directly relevant to their work, or see it exercising a passive influence, at most 65% of the 389 FBOs surveyed, suggesting, in turn, that the faith ethos of most charitable and development FBOs is compatible with the work of secularist donors, to the extent that the US pattern is evident in other parts of the world.

Table 1: The role of faith in the work of US service-provision FBOs.

Variable	Faith-based non-profits (n=303)(%)	Congregation Programmes (n=86) (%)	Total (%) (weighted)
Not relevant	22	9	19
Passive	46	45	46
Invitational	9	6	8
Relational	6	28	11
Integrated	16	11	15
Mandatory	1	1	1
Total	100	100	100

The Green and Sherman typology is useful in distinguishing between service-oriented FBOs but, given the range of organisations identified in Section 2 above, a broader, more encompassing typology is needed here. In general, we can distinguish between four main ways in which FBOs deploy faith through social or political engagement or link faith to developmental or humanitarian objectives:

Passive: Faith is subsidiary to broader humanitarian principles, as a motivation for action and in mobilising staff and supporters, and plays a secondary role to humanitarian considerations in identifying, helping or working with beneficiaries and partners.

Active: Faith provides an important and explicit motivation for action and in mobilising staff and supporters. It plays a direct role in identifying, helping or working with beneficiaries and partners, although there is no overt discrimination against non-believers and the organisation supports multi-faith cooperation.

Persuasive: Faith provides an important and explicit motivation for action and in mobilising staff and supporters. It plays a significant role in identifying, helping or working with beneficiaries and partners, provides the dominant basis for engagement, and aims to bring new converts to the faith or to advance the faith at the expense of others.

Exclusive: Faith provides the principal or overriding motivation for action and in mobilising staff and supporters. It provides the principal or sole consideration in identifying beneficiaries. Social and political engagement is rooted in the faith and is often militant or violent and directed against one or more rival faiths.

This typology highlights some of the dilemmas for donors who are concerned to understand and support the work of FBOs in development contexts, especially the work of charitable and development organisations. The first two variables (*passive* and *active*) present comparatively little difficulty for donors: here, faith motivates action, and therefore helps to mobilise staff, volunteers, members and supporters, but organisations do not expect a faith-based dividend (for instance, converts or greater credibility for the faith among people of other faiths). The other two variables (*persuasive* and *exclusive*) are more problematic, however, because they contain, to varying degrees, a commitment to winning new adherents to the faith (proselytising), providing support to the faithful to the exclusion of those of other faiths (i.e. direct or indirect discrimination) or advancing the cause of that faith at the expense of others, potentially generating conflict or social exclusion. Both clearly contain significant risks for donors.

Poverty: Malaise of Development

At present, donors support *passive* and *active* faith agendas in development contexts and often avoid support for *persuasive* and *exclusive* agendas.[18] Four key problems arise, however. Firstly, the four variables are not always clear-cut and exclusive; the policies and practices of an FBO may be *passive* or *active* on one issue, yet *persuasive* or *exclusive* on another. Secondly, FBOs are often highly networked and multi-purpose, and constituent parts may have different approaches to the deployment of faith. Thirdly, distinctions between *active* and *persuasive* stances, in particular, are culturally-nuanced and give rise to problems of interpretation. For instance, Western organisations (both governmental and non-governmental) that are working in Islamic cultural settings often work separately, yet in parallel, with Islamic FBOs which are local or originate in donor countries such as Saudi Arabia or Kuwait. Western organisations may find it difficult to distinguish between the *passive/active* and the *persuasive/ exclusive* among a range of Islamic charitable, representative or socio-political organisations and miss significant opportunities for productive partnership. Fourthly, FBOs which adopt a *persuasive* or *exclusive* stance may help large numbers of the poor and command their confidence, in part because of the religious or ethno-cultural bond that unites them.

These dilemmas become clearer when the work of FBOs is related to the typology. The *passive* stance, for instance, is most closely associated with development NGOs linked to the mainstream Christian churches. The work of FBOs affiliated to CIDSE, APRODEV and Caritas International, for instance, is inspired by Christian

---

[18] Prominent exceptions are the USA and Saudia Arabia. In both cases, significant sums of official funding are channelled through *persuasive* FBOs.

teachings, and these FBOs play an important role in mobilising the faith community in support of international development. They also rely heavily on church networks to work in developing countries with significant Christian communities. Faith-based principles, however, are secondary to broader humanitarian principles and they support the poor on a non-discriminatory basis in countries with large non-Christian populations, helping Christians and non-Christians on an equal basis.

The extent to which FBOs from other faith traditions adopt a similarly *passive* stance to the deployment of faith in development contexts has traditionally been less clear, although recent research is addressing this gap in knowledge. Wiktorowicz, (2001) and Clark, J. A., (2004) suggest that Islamic charitable FBOs wear their faith as lightly and unobtrusively as their Christian counterparts. According to Wiktorowicz, for instance, "the priority [for most Islamic NGOs in Jordan] is the services themselves, not a specific Islamic message or a political agenda":

> What differentiates Islamic NGOs from their secular counterparts is ... not the particular Islamic nature of their activities, but volunteers' belief that they are promoting Islam through their work. It is an insider belief in the mission, more than the activities themselves, that distinguishes them. (Wiktorowicz, 2001, p. 85)

The same is generally true for charitable and development organisations from other faith communities in Asia, Africa and Latin America, although government and non-governmental donors alike have much work to do in overcoming the institutional and cultural myopia that hinders engagement with them.

The *active* stance is evident in the work of different types of FBOs, including charitable and development organisations, representative organisations and missionary organisations. Globally, some development NGO networks, or mass membership organisations, employ a more fervent vision of Christian responsibility to help the poor. The UK-based Mothers' Union [MU], for instance, the world's largest Christian women's organisation with more than 3 million members, seeks "to strengthen and preserve marriage and Christian family life" and to "maintain a worldwide fellowship of Christians united in prayer ... and service".[19] It runs literacy and development programmes for women in sub-Saharan Africa, working through local MU groups. The MU, however, is committed to ecumenism, rather than conversion. MU staff members feel that its overt Christianity helps it to engage with women from other faith traditions, who mostly relate more readily to committed religious belief than to secularism.[20] Organisations such as the MU, therefore, wear their faith on the outside as well as the inside, but consequently have a significant ability to mobilise constituencies traditionally unmoved by secular development discourse. For donors, however, this *active* stance is problematic when transmitted through an organisation's policies, or where it dictates its approach to partnership. In such cases, dialogue between *active* FBOs and donors is often necessary to overcome misunderstandings or to clarify working assumptions.

Representative organisations and apex bodies necessarily adopt an *active* stance in their use of faith in development debates. To the extent that they represent the faithful, they wear their faith overtly, but they are *active* rather than *persuasive* to the extent in which they work

---

[19] See the Mothers' Union website: www.themothersunion.org . [Accessed July, 2005].
[20] B. Laws, Worldwide Projects Officer for the Mothers' Union (personal communication [telephone interview], November 25, 2004).

Faith Matters

closely with representative FBOs from other faith traditions to build inter-faith dialogue and cooperation. They ask policy-makers to acknowledge and respect the faith tradition, and therefore play an important role in promoting multiculturalism, but otherwise they seek no advantage for the faith community at the expense of others. As such, organisations such as the United States Council of Catholic Bishops, the Muslim Council of Great Britain or the National Council of Churches in the Philippines are important actors in the development process, educating and mobilising the faithful in support of development in international, national or sub-national settings and building the bridges to other faith traditions that reduce conflict and produce inclusive, multicultural societies.

Missionary organisations, however, also adopt an *active* stance in development contexts. Missionary orders associated with the mainstream Catholic and Protestant churches, for instance, have reconciled themselves over time to local faith discourses, including syncretism (the blending of established faith principles with local beliefs and customs). As such, they respond to local needs on the basis of faith principles, but otherwise avoid proselytising activities. Despite the proliferation of development NGOs, both secular and faith-based, such missionary organisations remain important actors in development contexts as providers of social services and as witnesses to the struggles of the poor. Often, they are closer to the poor than development NGOs, because they maintain a long-term presence in local communities and generally promote modest living and the sharing of privations that afflict the poor. They are frequently ignored, however, as civil society organisations and as relevant stakeholders in development contexts.

Poverty: Malaise of Development

The *persuasive* stance is primarily associated with missionary organisations of a different hue, charitable and development organisations, socio-political organisations and some representative organisations or apex bodies. Evangelical missionary organisations, in the case of Christianity, or Wahabi or Salafi-inspired organisations in the case of Islam, are associated with a fervent form of missionary zeal, an active campaign to win converts to the faith. The growth of US missionary evangelism, for instance, has produced "a new type of American missionary", trained in "strategic-level spiritual warfare", and equipped for "forays into enemy territory" (Moreau, Corwin & McGee, 2004, p. 289). Such missionary zeal is often evident, in different forms, in the work of evangelical Christian and Wahabi/Salafi-inspired development and charitable organisations. World Vision International, for example, is evangelical in its ethos and mission. WVI seeks converts to the faith among non-evangelical Christians and people of other, or no, faith; in Zimbabwe, for instance, field staff must sign a "statement of faith" as part of their contracts and evangelism committees are set up at project sites (Bornstein, 2002, p. 20, 15). According to Bornstein, such evangelism does not exclude non-Christians or non-evangelicals and brings positive development outcomes through the provision of long-term support to communities, including the empowerment of women trained to speak publicly and to preach. WVI attracts significant official donor funding, especially from USAID, but aspects of its ethos, including its overt proselytising and its emphasis on abstinence and faithfulness (rather than condom use) in the fight against HIV/AIDS, are problematic for some European donors.

Socio-political and representative organisations and apex bodies, on the other hand, are less interested in winning converts than in advancing the cause of the faith and increasing its political leverage or cultural resilience. Despite their commitment to proselytising and enhancing the position of their faith at the expense of others, *persuasive* organisations are potentially important partners in development contexts. The National Association of Evangelicals [NAE], for instance, sends thousands of missionaries around the world through the Evangelical Fellowship of Mission Agencies, yet also supports the US "Make Poverty History" campaign. In May 2005, British Prime Minister Tony Blair met the NAE President during a visit to Washington to lobby for support for UK proposals at the Gleneagles G7 summit, a recognition of the perceived importance of the NAE and its 40 milllion members to the "US Make Poverty History" campaign.

Organisations that deploy faith-based teachings in an *exclusive* way are also significant players in the context of development policy and discourse. UK-based World Jewish Relief, for instance, is *exclusive* in helping only Jewish communities in developing or transitional economies, and acts as the counterpart of the non-denominational World Jewish Aid (also based in the UK). At the opposite end of the spectrum are organisations that not only help the faith community, but work to advance the interests of the organisation and the faith in a sectarian manner, or to preserve socio-cultural values that isolate the faithful from mainstream society and from development interventions. Such organisations, however, are important in the context of development efforts. *Exclusive* (and *persuasive*) FBOs represent socially conservative religious currents that appeal to large numbers of adherents. Governments and donors face difficulties in connecting with these constituencies, and securing their support for policy initiatives in areas such as health, education and human rights, partly because of their perceived secularism and antipathy to matters of faith. However, engagement,

Poverty: Malaise of Development

wherever possible, with *persuasive* and *exclusive* FBOs provides opportunities to extend the reach of policy and practice and to make it more socially inclusive.

In India, for instance, prominent FBOs are committed to *Hindutva*, a sectarian form of Hindu nationalism. Collectively known as the *Sangh Parivar*, they include the *Bharatiya Janata Party* [BJP, or Indian Peoples Party], the *Rashtriya Swayamsevak Sangh* [RSS, or National Volunteers' Corps.], which is an all-male paramilitary organisation with an estimated 4.5 million members);[21] *Rashtra Sevika Samiti* (a women's organisation committed to traditional Hindu notions of femininity); and *Sewa Bharti* & *Sewa International*, the ostensibly charitable arms of the RSS. In practice, *Hindutva* organisations promote interfaith conflict through their support of sectarian Hindu causes (such as the destruction of the Babri Masjid Mosque in 1992) or their championing of the socially divisive institution of caste. In India, the major opposition to sectarian Hindu nationalism comes from secular nationalism, as represented by the Congress Party, and moderate Hindus see the electoral system as the primary means of opposing *Hindutva*. Two problems, however, arise for donors. Firstly, *Hindutva* is a malleable ideology and subject to different interpretations, not all of which are overtly sectarian or chauvinist. There is a possible role for donors in supporting these non-sectarian currents and building organisational capacity, but support of *Hindutva* organisations risks confrontation with the federal or state government, as well as alienating Indian secularists and foreign governments. The second problem is the absence of a well-organised middle ground between extreme Hindu

---

[21] 'Analysis: RSS Aims for a Hindu nation', *BBC News online* (at www.bbc.co.uk/news), March 10, 2003.

and secular nationalism, composed of moderate Hindu FBOs (committed to *passive* or *active* stances, as above). Many such organisations exist, mostly based on support for individual gurus.[22] A minority, for instance, actively oppose the institution of caste, but most simply refrain from supporting caste-based forms of social organisation. Organisations such as the Andhra Pradesh-based *Satya Sai Baba Society* (led by the guru Satya Sai Baba)[23] can have as many members as the RSS and a significant presence at state or federal level, but they lack the networks and commitment to political engagement of the *Sangh Parivar*. The question that arises, however, is whether or not there is a role for donors to work with state and federal governments to build the capacity of moderate Hindu FBOs, as a counterweight to the forces of extreme Hindu nationalism.

4. Conclusion

This question, of course, illustrates the significant challenges posed by the convergence of faith and development. Donor policy towards FBOs has traditionally been driven by established constitutional conventions on the separation of church and state. Faith-based organisations, however, have become important stakeholders in the development enterprise, challenging secular development discourse and policy. FBOs channel large volumes of money to the "developing" world from Europe, North America and the Middle East. They mobilise the faithful in support of international

---

[22] Most gurus derive support from followers who are not formally organised, although the more popular gurus have organised networks of support or oversee formal organisations.
[23] This organisation rejects caste and emphasises the equality of all, regardless of caste, creed, race or gender (Burnett, 2004, p. 179).

Poverty: Malaise of Development

development and they link migrants to the pan-national faith community. In Asia, Africa and Latin America, they provide vital services to the poor, helping them to organise to make governments accountable and so link governments and donors to communities alienated by secular discourse. Many FBOs, however, also promote social exclusion and conflict and oppose modern ideas that could help the poor and reduce their vulnerability. The difference between the "good" and the "bad" in the work of FBOs is evident in some circumstances, yet often it is difficult to elucidate, for instance, the difference between *active* and *persuasive* FBOs, or the "positive" and "negative" in the work of *persuasive* FBOs.[24]

Many of these phenomena are still not properly understood, largely because the development policy community ignored religion and faith until comparatively recently. The role of FBOs in channelling funding to developing countries, for instance, is still inadequately documented. Funding from the US Christian Right, or from groups and individuals in the Arab world who support the Wahabi form of Islam, represents significant financial flows to the developing world. Official Western donors and secular development NGOs, however, have an incomplete understanding of their impact; in particular, of the respects in which they represent a substantive countercurrent to the mainstream development enterprise or, alternatively, the extent to which they represent potential focuses for engagement.

To the extent that Western donors (multilateral, bilateral and non-governmental) support FBOs, they currently focus on *charitable and development organisations;* yet, as Section 2 argues, a wide range of FBOs act as drivers

---

[24] See Bornstein's (2002) discussion of World Vision on the latter dilemma.

of change in the developing world, including *representative organisations & apex bodies, socio-political organisations* and *missionary organisations*. Donors face significant challenges in engaging with this broader set of FBOs: of blurring church-state boundaries, of engaging with, or supporting, organisations which engage in discriminatory or sectarian practices, and of privileging some organisations at the expense of others. The rise of faith-based activism, however, makes it difficult for donors to ignore the broad range of FBOs examined above and donors face the challenge of devising strategies to engage with them; where appropriate, to network with them; to fund them; to build their capacity; and to engage in joint initiatives with them.

FBOs also differ enormously in the way they deploy faith in their pursuit of developmental, humanitarian, or broader political objectives. Donors have traditionally engaged with FBOs that deploy faith in a *passive* or *active* manner. Donors now face the challenge of selectively engaging with FBOs that use faith in a *persuasive* or *exclusive* manner, given their importance in channelling funding to developing countries, in providing services to the poor, and in representing them in different political forums. Donors have traditionally supported the forces of secular modernity over those of religious conservatism in contentious policy areas such as HIV/AIDS, reproductive rights or the empowerment of women. Increasingly, however, they face the challenge of building a middle ground of moderate faith-based praxis. 'Moderate', of course, is a relative concept in different regional or country contexts and one that straddles the *active, persuasive* and *exclusive* categories in Section 3. Whether European donors can engage with evangelical or Wahabi organisations that straddle the *active/persuasive* divide, or with the representatives of political Islam such as Hamas, remains to be seen. Whether or not donors can work with state or federal governments in India to support moderate forms of *Hindutva* through associated FBOs, or support moderate Hindu FBOs that respect minority faiths and challenge caste-based social exclusion, is similarly unclear.

These predicaments do not necessarily lend themselves to simple policy solutions. In India, for instance, some Hindu nationalist organisations mobilise women in a partially progressive manner; yet, for some Hindu nationalists, equal treatment of women is an anti-Muslim weapon (Keddie, 1998, p. 710). Nevertheless, engagement with FBOs which seem sectarian, chauvinistic or exclusionary has become a significant new challenge for development policy-makers. In the past, donors with a secular world view often failed to connect with, or even alienated, large groups of intended beneficiaries because of their failure to understand the faith tradition and its political and cultural import, or to acknowledge and engage with representative organisations. The challenge posed by the convergence of faith and development is to engage with faith discourses and associated organisations, which may seem counter-development or culturally exotic to a secular and technocratic worldview, in building the complex, multi-stakeholder partnerships increasingly central to the fight against global poverty. Put simply, in development contexts, *faith matters*!

References

Analysis: RSS aims for a Hindu nation, *BBC News online*. Retrieved March 10, 2003 from: www.bbc.co.uk/news

Bornstein, E. (2002). Developing faith: Theologies of economic development in Zimbabwe. *Journal of Religion in Africa, 32* (1), 4-31.

Burnett, D. (2004). The Satya Sai Baba Society. In Christopher Partridge (Ed.), *Encyclopedia of new religions: New religious movements, sects and alternative spiritualities* (pp. 179-80). Oxford: Lion.

Clark, J. A. (2004). *Islam, charity, and activism: Middle-class networks and social welfare in Egypt, Jordan, and Yemen.* Bloomington: Indiana University Press.

Clark, J. D. (2003). *Worlds apart: Civil society and the battle for ethical globalization.* London: Earthscan.

Clarke, G. (2006). Faith matters: Faith-based organisations, civil society and international development. *Journal of International Development, 18* (6), 835-48.

Collins, C. J. L., Gariyo, Z., & Burdon, T. (2001). Jubilee 2000: Citizen action across the North-South divide. In M. Edwards & J. Gaventa (Eds.), *Global citizen action* (pp. 135-48). London: Earthscan.

Department for International Development (2001). *Departmental report 2001: The Government's expenditure plans 2001/2002 to 2003/2004 and main estimates 2001/2002.* London: Stationery Office.

Poverty: Malaise of Development

Ellis, S., & Haar, G. ter. (2004). *Worlds of power: Religious thought and political practice in Africa*. New York: Oxford University Press.

Europa world yearbook 2004: Vol. 2. (2004). London: Europa Publications.

Green, J. C., & Sherman, A. L. (2002). *Fruitful collaborations: A survey of government-funded faith-based programs in 15 states*. Charlottesville, VA: Hudson Institute, Faith in Communities.

Hamas, Islamic Jihad (Palestinian Islamists), see Council on Foreign Relations, *Terrorism: Questions & Answers*, at: www.cfrterrorism.org/ groups/ hamas.html

Hearn, J. (2002). The 'invisible' NGO: US evangelical missions in Kenya. *Journal of Religion in Africa*, 32 (1), 32-60.

Keddie, N. R. (1998). The new religious politics: Where, when, and why do 'fundamentalisms' appear? *Comparative Studies in Society and History*, 40 (4), 696-723.

Kepel, G. (2001), *Jihad: The trail of political Islam* (A. F. Roberts, Trans.). London: I.B. Tauris.

Linden, I., Jawara, F., & Pingle, V. (2004). *Islam, DFID and poverty reduction: How to improve the partnership: report for the Department for International Development.* London: DFID.

Marshall, K., & Keough, L. (Eds.). (2004). *Mind, heart and soul in the fight against poverty.* Washington, DC: World Bank.

Mishal, S., & Sela, A. (2000). *The Palestinian Hamas: Vision, violence, and coexistence.* New York: Columbia University Press.

Moreau, A. S. (2000). Putting the survey in context. In J. A. Siewert & D. Welliver (Eds.), *Missions handbook: U.S. and Canadian ministries overseas 2001-2003* (pp. 33-80). Wheaton, IL: Evangelism and Missions Information Service.

Moreau, A. S., Corwin, G. R., & McGee, G. B. (2004). *Introducing world missions: A biblical, historical, and practical survey.* Grand Rapids, MI: Baker Academic.

Mothers' Union. About Mothers' Union. Retrieved July 2005 from: www.themothersunion.org

NOVIB (Oxfam Netherlands), & World Assembly of Muslim Youth (2004). Arab donor policies and practices on education in Somalia/land. Retrieved July 31, 2009, from: http://www.mbali.info/doc427.htm

Rosander, E. E., & Westerlund, D. (Eds.). (1997). *African Islam and Islam in Africa: Encounters between Sufis and Islamists*. London: Hurst.

Short, C. (2003). After September 11: What global development challenges lie ahead. In K. Marshall & R. Marsh (Eds.), *Millennium challenges for development and faith institutions* (pp. 3-11). Washington, DC: The World Bank.

Terrorism Undermines Political Islam in Indonesia, YaleGlobal online (www.yaleglobal.yale.edu), 26 November 2003.

Wallis, J. (2005). *God's politics: Why the right gets it wrong and the left doesn't get it*. San Francisco: HarperSanFrancisco.

Wiktorowicz, Q. (2001). *The management of Islamic activism: Salafis, the Muslim Brotherhood, and state power in Jordan*. Albany: State University of New York Press.

Wuthnow, R. (2004). *Saving America?: Faith-based services and the future of civil society*. Princeton, NJ: Princeton University Press.